A Devotion Guide

In Your
Heart & Soul

By: Kaitlyn King

Dedication:

To Mom –

You have taught me more than you will ever know.

Thank you for always loving and supporting me!

In Your Heart and Soul

An Introductory Guide to Devotions

366 Bible Passages

Guided Bible Study and Prayer Prompts

<u>You will need:</u>

- Bible
- Writing Utensils
- Highlighter

"Therefore shall ye lay up these my words in your heart and in your soul,"
Deuteronomy 11:18a

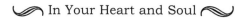 In Your Heart and Soul

Day 1: Genesis 1:1 – 2:3

Bible Study:

➤ Underline the word firmament and define it using a dictionary. Answer:

_____

➤ List what was created on each day:

1. _____

2. _____

3. _____

4. _____

5. _____

6. _____

7. _____

Prayer Prompts:

➤ Praise God for something beautiful in nature.

➤ Pray for a miracle you want to see.

Day 2: Genesis 2:7 – 15

Bible Study:

➤ How was man formed? _____

➤ What was man's purpose? _____

➤ List the three types of trees:

1. _____

2. _____

3. _____

Prayer Prompts:

➤ Praise God for creating you for a purpose.

➤ Pray for the world. Pray for its problems, needs, or whatever God leads you to pray for.

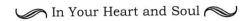

Day 3: Genesis 2:16 – 24

Bible Study:

➢ Put a star next to the command.

➢ How was woman formed? _____

➢ Why was woman formed? _____

➢ Underline and define words you do not know.

_____

_____

_____

Prayer Prompts:

➢ Praise God for people that have met needs in your life.

➢ Pray for these people

➢ Pray for your spouse or future spouse.

Day 4: Genesis 3:1 - 24

Bible Study:

➢ Underline and define words you do not know.

_____

_____

_____

➢ Put an exclamation point (!) next to what Adam and Eve did wrong and an (X) next to what happened because of their actions.

➢ Place a box around each action word.

Prayer Prompts:

➢ Praise God for His mercy and correction.

➢ Confess (Ask for forgiveness) for something you have done wrong.

➢ Pray for God to show you how to avoid repeating your sin.

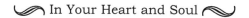

Day 5: Genesis 4:1 – 16

Bible Study:

➢ Underline and define words you do not know.

_____

_____

_____

➢ Put an exclamation point (!) next to what Cain did wrong and an (X) next to what happened because of his actions.

➢ What was Cain's offering? _____

➢ What was Abel's offering? _____

➢ Why wasn't Cain's offering accepted? _____

Prayer Prompts:

➢ Praise God for your family members.

➢ Ask forgiveness for times you have been frustrated and angry at your family members.

➢ Pray for your family members and your relationships with them.

Day 6: Genesis 6:5 – 22

Bible Study:

➢ Underline and define words you do not know.

_____

_____

_____

➢ Put an arrow next to an act of grace.

➢ Double underline God's promise for the future.

➢ Circle the act of obedience.

Prayer Prompts:

➢ Praise God for an act of grace in your life.

➢ Pray for a project you are working on.

➢ Pray for salvation for people in your city.

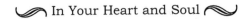

Day 7: Genesis 7:1 – 16

Bible Study:

➢ Who went on the ark? _____

➢ How many of each animal went on the ark?

_____

➢ Why did they bring more of the clean animals?

_____

➢ How many days did it rain? _____

➢ Circle the act of faith.

Prayer Prompts:

➢ Praise God for how He has provided for you.

➢ Confess something you are feeling guilty about.

➢ Pray for faith to follow God's leading in your life.

Day 8: Genesis 8:1 – 21

Bible Study:

➢ What birds did Noah release and why?

_____

➢ Place a box around God's actions.

➢ Double underline God's promise.

➢ How did Noah thank God for saving him?

_____

Prayer Prompts:

➢ Praise God for saving you.

➢ Pray for God to help you as you go through a time of struggles and fear.

Day 9: Genesis 9: 8 – 18

Bible Study:

➤ What promise did God make? _____

➤ What is the sign of His promise? _____

➤ Underline and define words you do not know.

_____

_____

_____

➤ Double underline God's promise.

➤ Highlight a passage that speaks to you.

Prayer Prompts:

➤ Praise God for keeping promises in your life.

➤ Confess times you have forgotten God's promise to take care of you.

➤ Pray for faith to trust God more in your life.

Day 10: Genesis 11:1 – 9

Bible Study:

➤ Underline and define words you do not know.

_____

_____

➤ Put an exclamation point (!) next to what the people did wrong and an (X) next to what happened because of their actions.

➤ Why did God confuse their languages?

_____

Prayer Prompts:

➤ Praise God for being invested in your life.

➤ Confess acts of pride in your life.

➤ Pray for God to correct your bad habits.

Day 11: Job 1:1 – 22

Bible Study:

➢ Underline and define words you do not know.

_____

_____

_____

➢ Double underline God's words.

➢ Put an exclamation point (!) next to what Satan did.

➢ Put an (X) next to Job's reaction.

Prayer Prompts:

➢ Praise God for His protection in your life.

➢ Confess loving material things.

➢ Pray for God to help you avoid evil.

Day 12: Job 2:1 – 10

Bible Study:

➢ Underline and define words you do not know.

_____

_____

_____

➢ Double underline God's words.

➢ Put an exclamation point (!) next to Job's wife's reaction.

➢ Put an (X) next to Job's reaction.

Prayer Prompts:

➢ Praise God for having control over the universe.

➢ Confess anger towards God.

➢ Pray for integrity.

Day 13: Job 2:11 – 13, 4:1 – 8, 8:1 – 20, & 11:1 – 20

Bible Study:

➢ Underline and define words you do not know.

_____

_____

_____

➢ List Job's friends and what they though Job did wrong:

1. _____

2. _____

3. _____

➢ Had Job sinned against God? _____

Prayer Prompts:

➢ Praise God for being just.

➢ Confess judging others.

➢ Pray for your friends.

Day 14: Job 42: 1 – 17

Bible Study:

➢ Underline and define words you do not know.

_____

_____

_____

➢ Double underline God's words.

➢ Double star the blessing Job received.

Prayer Prompts:

➢ Praise God for blessings you have received.

➢ Confess bitterness towards your friends.

➢ Pray for a blessing you would like to receive.

Day 15: Genesis 12:1 – 9

Bible Study:

- Double underline God's words.
- Circle acts of obedience.
- Why did Abram leave his home? _____
- How would you feel if God told you to leave your home and not know where you were going?

  _____

  _____

Prayer Prompts:

- Praise God for His leading in your life.
- Confess your fears.
- Pray for your future.

Day 16: Genesis 13:1 – 18

Bible Study:

- What was the problem? _____
- What was Abram's solution?

  _____

- Did Lot make the right choice and why?

  _____

  _____

- Double underline God's promises.
- Put a star next to God's command.
- Circle Abram's obedience.

Prayer Prompts:

- Praise God for His promises.
- Confess times you acted without God's leading.
- Pray for a family member that is away from the Lord.

Day 17: Genesis 18:1 – 15

Bible Study:

➤ How did Abraham prepare for the Lord's visit?

_____

➤ What was Sarah's reaction to hearing she would have a baby at an old age?

_____

➤ Underline and define words you do not know.

_____

_____

➤ Double underline God's promise.
➤ Highlight the first question in verse 14.

Prayer Prompts:

➤ Praise God for something miraculous He has done in your life.
➤ Confess a time you did not believe God could do something in your life.
➤ Pray to see a miracle in your life.

Day 18: Genesis 21:1 – 6, 22 ;1 – 14

Bible Study:

➤ How old was Abraham when God gave him Isaac? _____
➤ How would you feel if God asked you to do this?

_____

➤ Circle the act of faith.
➤ Why do you think God asked this of Abraham?

_____

➤ What is this a picture of that happens in the New Testament? _____
➤ Highlight a passage that speaks to you.

Prayer Prompts:

➤ Praise God for the trials in your life.
➤ Confess acts of disobedience.
➤ Pray for the salvation of a loved one.

Day 19: Genesis 24:1 – 26

Bible Study:

- ➤ Put boxes around the actions.
- ➤ What was the servant's job? _____
- ➤ Highlight the servant's prayer.
- ➤ Put a squiggle line under how the servant praised God.

Prayer Prompts:

- ➤ Praise God for an answered prayer.
- ➤ Confess a worry you have.
- ➤ Pray for a stranger you noticed today.

Day 20: Genesis 24:48 – 67

Bible Study:

- ➤ Put a squiggle line under acts of worship to the Lord.
- ➤ How would you feel if you had to marry a stranger?

  _____

- ➤ Highlight a passage that speaks to you.

Prayer Prompts:

- ➤ Praise God for the people He brings into your life.
- ➤ Confess fear of following His will for your life.
- ➤ Pray for a relationship that will be coming soon in your life.

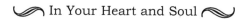

Day 21: Genesis 25:19 – 34

Bible Study:

➤ Underline and define words you do not know.

_____

_____

_____

➤ What was wrong with Esau? _____

➤ How did Jacob get the birthright?

_____

➤ Which brother did wrong?

_____

_____

Prayer Prompts:

➤ Praise God for the ways your family shows you their love.

➤ Confess times when you acted in haste.

➤ Pray for someone you do not get along with.

Day 22: Genesis 26:12 – 33

Bible Study:

➤ Underline and define words you do not know.

_____

_____

➤ How would you react in Isaac's position?

_____

➤ How did God bless Isaac? _____

➤ Double underline God's promise.

Prayer Prompts:

➤ Praise God for conflicts.

➤ Confess your anger.

➤ Pray for God to help you with confrontations.

Day 23: Genesis 27:1 – 35

Bible Study:

➤ Underline and define words you do not know.

_____

_____

_____

➤ Put an exclamation point (!) next to Jacob's actions.

➤ Put an (X) next to what happened to Jacob because of his actions.

➤ How do you think Jacob's actions changed his relationships with his family?

_____

Prayer Prompts:

➤ Praise God for forgiving your past.

➤ Confess a wrong you have done to someone else.

➤ Pray for a blessing God has specifically for you.

Day 24: Genesis 28:10 – 22

Bible Study:

➤ Double underline God's promise.

➤ Put a squiggle line under how Jacob worshiped.

➤ What did Jacob see in his dream?

_____

➤ What was Jacob's reaction to his dream?

_____

Prayer Prompts:

➤ Praise God for His plans for your future.

➤ Confess sins you committed today.

➤ Pray for the faith to follow God's leading in your life.

Day 25: Genesis 29:1 – 14

Bible Study:

➢ Underline and define words you do not know.

_____

_____

_____

➢ What was Jacob's connection to Rachel?

_____

➢ Describe their meeting in your own words.

_____

_____

➢ Write down any questions you have for your pastor.

_____

_____

Prayer Prompts:

➢ Praise God for your family.

➢ Confess feelings of bitterness towards someone that you are withholding forgiveness from.

➢ Pray for God to bring the right people into your life.

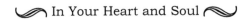

Day 26: Genesis 29:15 – 30

Bible Study:

➢ Look up the phrase "tender eyed." _____

_____

➢ Put an exclamation point (!) next to the act of deceit.

➢ How was Laban's actions like Jacob's actions towards Esau?

_____

_____

➢ How many years did Jacob end up working for Rachel? _____

Prayer Prompts:

➢ Praise God for His protection in your life.

➢ Confess an act of deceit you have done.

➢ Pray for someone you know that has been mistreated.

Day 27: Genesis 30:25 – 42

Bible Study:

➢ Underline and define words you do not know.

_____

_____

_____

➢ Box Jacob's actions.

➢ How did God bless Jacob?

_____

_____

Prayer Prompts:

➢ Praise God for His blessings in your life.

➢ Confess times when you have forgotten to be thankful for the blessings God has given you.

➢ Pray for someone in your life to receive a special blessing.

Day 28: Genesis 33:1 – 20

Bible Study:

- ➤ Put an arrow next to an act of forgiveness.

- ➤ Circle Jacob's apology.

- ➤ Put a squiggle line under how Jacob thanked God.

- ➤ Write about a time you were forgiven by someone.

  _____

  _____

- ➤ Write about a time you forgave someone.

  _____

  _____

Prayer Prompts:

- ➤ Praise God for forgiveness.

- ➤ Confess a sin you committed against someone. Ask God to lead you to make things right with that person.

- ➤ Pray for God to help you reconcile with an old friend or family member you haven't seen for a while.

Day 29: Genesis 37:1 – 11

Bible Study:

- ➤ Put an exclamation point (!) next to the sin.

- ➤ Double underline God's prophecy through Joseph's dreams.

- ➤ What do you think the dreams mean?

  _____

  _____

Prayer Prompts:

- ➤ Praise God for His plans for your future.

- ➤ Confess any bad feelings you have for your family members.

- ➤ Pray for God to show you His will for your life.

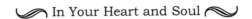

Day 30: Genesis 37:12 – 36

Bible Study:

➤ Underline and define words you do not know.

_____

_____

_____

➤ Put an exclamation point (!) next to the brother's actions.
➤ How would you feel in Joseph's place?

_____

_____

Prayer Prompts:

➤ Praise God for the trials in your life.
➤ Confess a time you hurt a family member.
➤ Pray for your siblings (or friends that have been like siblings.) Pray for their health, needs, and future.

Day 31: Genesis 39:1 – 20

Bible Study:

➤ Underline and define words you do not know.

_____

_____

➤ Put an arrow next to God's grace in Joseph's life.
➤ Put an exclamation point (!) next to the sins in this passage.
➤ How would you feel about being falsely accused?

_____

_____

Prayer Prompts:

➤ Praise God for His grace in your life.
➤ Confess a lie you have told.
➤ Pray for God to protect you from false accusations.

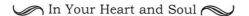

Day 32: Genesis 39:20 – 40:23

Bible Study:

➢ Underline and define words you do not know.

_____

_____

_____

➢ Double underline the prophetic dreams.

➢ Put an arrow next to how God blessed Joseph in prison.

Prayer Prompts:

➢ Praise God for His blessings during the hard times.

➢ Confess a time when you forgot a blessing someone gave you. Strive to thank that person for the blessing.

➢ Pray for God to lay someone on your heart that could use a blessing.

Day 33: Genesis 41:1 – 40

Bible Study:

➢ Double underline Pharaoh's prophetic dreams.

➢ Put an arrow next to how God blessed Joseph in prison.

➢ Put a star next to Joseph's wise suggestion.

Prayer Prompts:

➢ Praise God for His timing.

➢ Confess feelings of impatience.

➢ Pray for patience.

Day 34: Genesis 42:1 – 25

Bible Study:

➢ Underline and define words you do not know.

_____

_____

_____

➢ How do you think Joseph felt seeing his brothers again after so many years?

_____

➢ What do you think of Joseph's actions?

_____

Prayer Prompts:

➢ Praise God for forgiveness.

➢ Confess an old sin you never confessed.

➢ Pray for a graceful and merciful attitude.

Day 35: Genesis 43:1 – 23

Bible Study:

➢ Underline and define words you do not know.

_____

_____

_____

➢ Put a squiggle line under the names of God.

➢ Write your thoughts about this passage.

_____

_____

Prayer Prompts:

➢ Praise God for how He provides for your family.

➢ Confess sins you committed today.

➢ Pray for God to meet your daily needs.

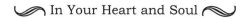

Day 36: Genesis 44:1 – 34

Bible Study:

➢ Place boxes around the actions.

➢ What do you think of Joseph's actions?

_____

➢ What do you think of the brother's actions?

_____

➢ Have the brothers changed? _____

Prayer Prompts:

➢ Praise God for how He provides for your family.

➢ Confess sins you committed today.

➢ Pray for God to meet your daily needs.

Day 37: Genesis 45:1 – 15

Bible Study:

➢ Place an arrow next to the act of forgiveness.

➢ Circle the ways God took care of Joseph.

➢ Highlight a passage that speaks to you.

Prayer Prompts:

➢ Praise God for redemption and second chances.

➢ Confess times you were slow to forgive.

➢ Pray for a friend you have lost touch with.

Day 38: Genesis 45:25 – 46:4 & 46:29 – 31

Bible Study:

➤ Put a squiggle line under how Israel praised God.

➤ Double underline God's words to Israel.

➤ Rewrite Israel and Joseph's reunion in your own words:

_____

_____

_____

_____

_____

_____

_____

Prayer Prompts:

➤ Praise God for an answered prayer that you have been praying about for many years.

➤ Confess feeling impatient with God.

➤ Pray for something you think is impossible.

Day 39: Exodus 1:6 – 22

Bible Study:

➤ Put an exclamation point (!) next to Pharaoh's evil plan.

➤ What was Pharaoh's fear? _____

➤ How were the midwives brave?

_____

➤ Put an arrow next to how God blessed the midwives.

Prayer Prompts:

➤ Praise God for brave people in your community.

➤ Confess your fears of standing up for God.

➤ Pray for God to show you ways to make a difference in your community.

Day 40: Exodus 2:1 – 10

Bible Study:

➤ Put a box around the actions of Moses' mom.

➤ List the three women in this passage and how each of them were brave in their own way:

_____

_____

_____

➤ How did God protect Moses?

_____

_____

_____

Prayer Prompts:

➤ Praise God for how He has protected you.

➤ Confess a sin you committed this week.

➤ Pray for courage.

Day 41: Exodus 2:11 – 22

Bible Study:

➤ Put an exclamation point (!) next to the bad actions.

➤ Put an X next to the result of Moses' actions.

➤ Put an arrow next to Moses' good actions.

Prayer Prompts:

➤ Praise God for being merciful.

➤ Confess doing the wrong thing for the "right" reason.

➤ Pray for a merciful attitude toward others.

Day 42: Exodus 3:1 – 20

Bible Study:

➢ Underline and define words you do not know.

_____

_____

_____

➢ Double underline God's words.

➢ Highlight a passage that speaks to you.

Prayer Prompts:

➢ Praise God for speaking to you.

➢ Confess running away from your problems.

➢ Pray for God to deliver you from your enemies.

Day 43: Exodus 4:1 – 18

Bible Study:

➢ Put an exclamation point (!) next to Moses' doubts.

➢ Double underline God's words.

➢ Why was God angry with Moses?

_____

_____

_____

Prayer Prompts:

➢ Praise God for His will for your life.

➢ Confess your doubts.

➢ Pray for God to prepare you for His will.

Day 44: Exodus 7:8 – 25

Bible Study:

➤ Double underline God's words.

➤ Circle Aaron's obedience.

➤ Put an X next to what happened when Aaron obeyed.

➤ Put an exclamation point (!) next to the sorcerer's response.

Prayer Prompts:

➤ Praise God that He is stronger than the world.

➤ Confess your fears to Him.

➤ Pray that you will not be convinced by false prophets.

Day 45: Exodus 8:1 – 32

Bible Study:

➤ Double underline God's words.

➤ What are the plagues we have read about so far?

_____

_____

_____

_____

➤ How does the sorcerer's reaction mirror what non-believers do today?

_____

_____

_____

➤ Put an X next to what happened when Aaron obeyed.

Prayer Prompts:

➤ Praise God for a miracle you see in nature.

➤ Confess times you try to do things in your own strength.

➤ Pray for someone with a hardened heart.

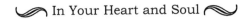

Day 46: Exodus 9:1 – 35

Bible Study:

➤ Double underline God's words.

➤ Box God's actions.

➤ How does the sorcerer's reaction mirror what non-believers do today?

_____

_____

_____

➤ Put an exclamation point (!) next to Pharaoh's reactions.

Prayer Prompts:

➤ Praise God for His persistence.

➤ Confess ignoring God's warnings.

➤ Pray for the leader of your country.

Day 47: Exodus 10:1 – 29

Bible Study:

➤ Double underline God's words.

➤ Box God's actions.

➤ What are all the plagues so far?

_____

_____

_____

_____

➤ Why do you think God hardened Pharaoh's heart?

_____

_____

Prayer Prompts:

➤ Praise God for a miracle in your life.

➤ Confess times when you had a hard heart.

➤ Pray for God's leading in your life.

Day 48: Exodus 11:1 – 10 & 12:21 – 31

Bible Study:

➤ Double underline God's words.

➤ Circle the children of Israel's obedience.

➤ Put an X next to what happened to the first born of each household.

Prayer Prompts:

➤ Praise God for Salvation.

➤ Confess a sin you continue to do.

➤ Pray for your neighbor's salvation.

Day 49: Exodus 14:5 – 31

Bible Study:

➤ Double underline God's words.

➤ Box Pharaoh's actions.

➤ Put an exclamation point (!) next to the doubts of the Israelites.

➤ Put two stars next to the miracle.

➤ Put an X next to what happened to Pharaoh.

Prayer Prompts:

➤ Praise God for His power.

➤ Confess your doubts.

➤ Pray for God to deliver you from your enemies.

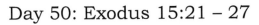

Day 50: Exodus 15:21 – 27

Bible Study:

- ➤ Look up a map showing where they were.
- ➤ What does Marah mean? _____
- ➤ Put an exclamation point (!) next to what the people did wrong.
- ➤ What made the waters sweet?

_____

_____

_____

Prayer Prompts:

- ➤ Praise God for something sweet in your life.
- ➤ Confess your bitterness.
- ➤ Pray for God to help you to stop complaining.

Day 51: Exodus 16:1 – 17

Bible Study:

- ➤ Double underline God's words.
- ➤ Put an exclamation point (!) next to the Israelites' sin.
- ➤ How did God provide for them in the wilderness?

_____

_____

_____

- ➤ What is Manna?

_____

Prayer Prompts:

- ➤ Praise God for His provision.
- ➤ Confess your frustrations to God.
- ➤ Pray for God to meet your daily needs.

Day 52: Exodus 17:1 – 7

Bible Study:

- ➤ Double underline God's words.

- ➤ Put an exclamation point (!) next to the Israelites' sin.

- ➤ What miracle did God perform?

  _____

- ➤ Why did Moses name the place Massah and Merbah?

  _____

  _____

Prayer Prompts:

- ➤ Praise God for His corrections.

- ➤ Confess times you have tempted the Lord.

- ➤ Pray for God to protect you daily.

Day 53: Exodus 19:20 – 20:17

Bible Study:

- ➤ Underline and define words you do not know.

  _____

  _____

  _____

- ➤ Double underline God's words.

- ➤ Star each of the ten commandments.

- ➤ Why were they given the 10 commandments?

  _____

  _____

- ➤ Memorize the ten commandments.

Prayer Prompts:

- ➤ Praise God for clear commandments.

- ➤ Confess times the commandment you break the most.

- ➤ Pray for God to help you keep the commandments.

Day 54: Exodus 32:1 – 26

Bible Study:

- ➢ Put an exclamation point (!) next to the people's sin.
- ➢ Double underline God's words.
- ➢ Box Moses' actions.
- ➢ Highlight the question in verse 26.

Prayer Prompts:

- ➢ Praise God for the Bible.
- ➢ Confess your fear.
- ➢ Pray for God to show you how to be on the Lord's side.
- ➢ Pray for something you need today.

Day 55: Numbers 13:1 – 22 & 25 – 33

Bible Study:

- ➢ Double underline God's words.
- ➢ What were the two reports?

_____

_____

- ➢ What was waiting for them in the Promised Land?

_____

_____

_____

_____

Prayer Prompts:

- ➢ Praise God for His plans for you.
- ➢ Confess your doubt.
- ➢ Pray for faith to claim God's promises.
- ➢ Pray for something you need today.

Day 56: Numbers 21:4 – 9

Bible Study:

➢ Double underline God's words.

➢ Put an exclamation point (!) next to what the people did wrong.

➢ Put an X next to what happened to them.

➢ Circle the people's obedience.

➢ Highlight the last part of verse 9.

Prayer Prompts:

➢ Praise God for healing.

➢ Confess a sin that you repeatedly do.

➢ Pray for God to heal someone that is sick.

➢ Pray for something you need today.

Day 57: Numbers 22:1 – 35

Bible Study:

➢ Double underline God's words.

➢ Star God's commands.

➢ Put an exclamation point (!) next to Balaam's disobedience.

➢ Put two stars next to the miracle.

➢ Circle Balaam's repentance.

Prayer Prompts:

➢ Praise God for second chances.

➢ Confess your disobedience.

➢ Pray for God to soften your heart.

➢ Pray for something you need today.

Day 58: Exodus 17:8 – 16

Bible Study:

➢ Double underline God's instructions.

➢ Put an arrow next to Aaron and Hur's support and encouragement.

➢ Double star the miracle.

➢ Put a squiggle line under Moses' praise and worship.

➢ Highlight a passage that speaks to you.

Prayer Prompts:

➢ Praise God supportive friends.

➢ Confess a sin God has laid on your heart.

➢ Pray for your friends.

➢ Pray for something you need today.

Day 59: Joshua 1:1 – 9

Bible Study:

➢ Double underline God's words and promises.

➢ Highlight the first parts of verses 6, 7, and 9.

➢ Why do you think God repeated this?

_____

_____

_____

_____

Prayer Prompts:

➢ Praise God for His promises. (Be specific)

➢ Confess your fears.

➢ Pray for courage.

➢ Pray for something you need today.

Day 60: Joshua 2:1 – 24

Bible Study:

➤ Put an arrow next to Rahab's kindness.

➤ Highlight verse 24.

➤ Why did Rahab help them?

_____

_____

_____

_____

Prayer Prompts:

➤ Praise God for His power. (Be specific)

➤ Confess your doubts. (Be specific)

➤ Pray for someone in another country.

➤ Pray for something you need today.

Day 61: Joshua 3:1 – 4:8

Bible Study:

➤ Double underline God's instructions.

➤ Circle the Israelites obedience.

➤ Double star the miracle.

➤ Put a squiggle line under how they praised God.

Prayer Prompts:

➤ Praise God for miracles. (Be specific)

➤ Confess your forgetting God's goodness in your life. (Be specific)

➤ Pray that God will show you mighty things.

➤ Pray for something you need today.

Day 62: Joshua 6:2 – 25

Bible Study:

- ➤ Double underline God's instructions.
- ➤ Circle the people's obedience.
- ➤ Double star the miracle.
- ➤ Put an arrow next to the act of mercy for Rahab.

Prayer Prompts:

- ➤ Praise God for how He has used you.
- ➤ Confess a sin God has laid on your heart.
- ➤ Pray that God to show you mercy.
- ➤ Pray for something you need today.

Day 63: Joshua 7:1 – 11, 16 – 26

Bible Study:

- ➤ Double underline God's words.
- ➤ Put an exclamation point (!) next to Achan's sin.
- ➤ Put an X next to the consequences for Achan's sin.

Prayer Prompts:

- ➤ Praise God for clear instructions.
- ➤ Confess a sin God has laid on your heart.
- ➤ Pray for someone struggling with sin.
- ➤ Pray for something you need today.

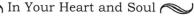

Day 64: Joshua 8:1 – 21

Bible Study:

➢ Double underline God's words.

➢ Circle Joshua's obedience.

➢ Put a box around the battle.

➢ Why did God give them the victory this time?

_____

_____

_____

Prayer Prompts:

➢ Praise God for a victory in your life.

➢ Confess a sin God has laid on your heart.

➢ Pray for someone that needs a victory in their life.

➢ Pray for something you need today.

Day 65: Joshua 9:3 – 27

Bible Study:

➢ Put an exclamation point (!) next to the Gibeonite's deceitful actions.

➢ Put an X next to what happened to them.

➢ How could Joshua have changed these events?

_____

_____

_____

Prayer Prompts:

➢ Praise God for prayer.

➢ Confess acting without praying first.

➢ Pray for wisdom.

➢ Pray for something you need today.

Day 66: Joshua 10:1 – 21

Bible Study:

➤ Put boxes around the actions.

➤ Double star the miracle.

➤ Double underline God's words.

Prayer Prompts:

➤ Praise God for a victory in your life.

➤ Confess anger toward someone.

➤ Pray for someone that has wronged you.

➤ Pray for something you need today.

Day 67: Joshua 14: 6 – 13

Bible Study:

➤ Highlight the first part of verse 12.

➤ What "mountain" has God promised you?

_____

_____

_____

➤ Do you still have the desire to go get that mountain?

_____

_____

_____

Prayer Prompts:

➤ Praise God for the goals He has given to you.

➤ Confess your reasons for not accomplishing the goals God gave to you.

➤ Pray for determination.

➤ Pray for something you need today.

Day 68: Judges 3:12 – 31

Bible Study:

- ➤ Put an exclamation point (!) next to verse 12.
- ➤ Put an X next to what God did to punish them.
- ➤ Put an arrow next to the man God raised up.
- ➤ Box Ehud's actions.

Prayer Prompts:

- ➤ Praise God for your pastor.
- ➤ Confess a repeated sin.
- ➤ Pray for your pastor.
- ➤ Pray for something you need today.

Day 69: Judges 4:1 – 15

Bible Study:

- ➤ Put an exclamation point (!) next to what the Israelites did wrong.
- ➤ Put an X next to how God punished them.
- ➤ Put an arrow next to the woman God raised up.
- ➤ Box Deborah's actions.

Prayer Prompts:

- ➤ Praise God for a godly lady you know.
- ➤ Confess a repeated sin.
- ➤ Pray for the godly lady.
- ➤ Pray for something you need today.

Day 70: Judges 4:17 – 24 & 5:24 – 27

Bible Study:

- ➢ Box the actions.
- ➢ Highlight a passage that speaks to you.
- ➢ Write a thought God gave you while reading this passage.

_____

_____

_____

Prayer Prompts:

- ➢ Praise God for using you.
- ➢ Confess self-doubt.
- ➢ Pray for courage.
- ➢ Pray for something you need today.

Day 71: Judges 6:11 – 32

Bible Study:

- ➢ Double underline God's words.
- ➢ Put an exclamation point (!) next to what the Israelites did wrong.
- ➢ Box the signs.
- ➢ Put a squiggle line under how Gideon praised God.
- ➢ Highlight a passage that speaks to you.

Prayer Prompts:

- ➢ Praise God for His patience.
- ➢ Confess moments of unbelief.
- ➢ Pray for God to make His will clear to you.
- ➢ Pray for something you need today.

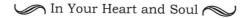

Day 72: Judges 6:33 – 7:8

Bible Study:

- ➤ Double underline God's words.
- ➤ Box the signs God gave.
- ➤ Was Gideon wrong to ask for a sign? Explain your answer.

_____

_____

_____

- ➤ Why did God only want 300 people?

_____

_____

Prayer Prompts:

- ➤ Praise God for a sign He has given to you.
- ➤ Confess any unbelief you have in His power.
- ➤ Pray for God to show you a miracle.
- ➤ Pray for something you need today.

Day 73: Judges 7:9 – 24

Bible Study:

- ➤ Double underline God's words.
- ➤ Double star the miracle.
- ➤ How did God alleviate Gideon's fears?

_____

_____

_____

Prayer Prompts:

- ➤ Praise God for His comfort.
- ➤ Confess your fears.
- ➤ Pray for God to remove your fears.
- ➤ Pray for something you need today.

Day 74: Judges 13:1 – 4, 24 & 15:4 – 5

Bible Study:

➢ Put an exclamation point (!) next to the first verse.

➢ Put an exclamation point (!) next to Sampson's sinful act.

➢ If Sampson was supposed to be a man of God, how could he have done sinful things? Explain your answer.

_____

_____

_____

Prayer Prompts:

➢ Praise God for His leading.

➢ Confess a sin no one knows about.

➢ Pray for God to protect Christian leaders.

➢ Pray for something you need today.

Day 75: Judges 15:9 – 17

Bible Study:

➢ Double star the miracle.

➢ What strange weapon did Sampson use?

➢ Put an exclamation point (!) next to Philistine's plan.

Prayer Prompts:

➢ Praise God for giving you strength.

➢ Confess evil thoughts toward someone else.

➢ Pray for God to protect you from your enemies.

➢ Pray for something you need today.

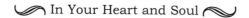

Day 76: Judges 16:4 – 21

Bible Study:

➤ Put an exclamation point (!) next to Philistine's plan.

➤ Put an exclamation point (!) next to Delilah's deceit.

➤ Where did Sampson's strength come from? _____

➤ Why didn't Sampson know the strength of God had left him?

_____

_____

_____

Prayer Prompts:

➤ Praise God for His power.

➤ Confess doing things without God's power.

➤ Pray for strength.

➤ Pray for something you need today.

Day 77: Judges 16:22 – 30

Bible Study:

➤ Double star the miracle.

➤ What did you learn from the life of Sampson?

_____

_____

_____

_____

_____

Prayer Prompts:

➤ Praise God for the Bible.

➤ Confess your failures.

➤ Pray for God to give you another chance.

➤ Pray for something you need today.

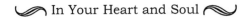

Day 78: Ruth 1:1 – 22

Bible Study:

➢ Look up a map of this area.

➢ What does Mara mean? _____

➢ List each of the characters and a trat that describes them:

_____

_____

_____

_____

_____

Prayer Prompts:

➢ Praise God for never leaving you.

➢ Confess any bitterness you have.

➢ Pray for God to heal your soul.

➢ Pray for something you need today.

Day 79: Ruth 2:1 – 23

Bible Study:

➢ Put an arrow next to the acts of kindness.

➢ Box Ruth's actions.

➢ Highlight verse 20.

➢ Compare the change in Naomi's behavior in chapters 1-2.

_____

_____

_____

Prayer Prompts:

➢ Praise God for His patience.

➢ Confess taking time to get over bitterness.

➢ Pray for a new beginning in your life.

➢ Pray for something you need today.

Day 80: Ruth 3:1 – 6 & 4:1 – 15

Bible Study:

➤ Circle Ruth's obedience.

➤ Put an X next to the result of Ruth's obedience.

➤ Highlight a passage that speaks to you.

➤ What thought did God give you while reading this passage.

_____

_____

_____

_____

Prayer Prompts:

➤ Praise God for His rewards.

➤ Confess disobedience.

➤ Pray for something you want in the future.

➤ Pray for something you need today.

Day 81: 1 Samuel 1:1 – 20

Bible Study:

➤ Underline and define words you do not know.

_____

_____

_____

➤ Put a squiggle line under Hannah's prayer.

➤ Double underline the answer to her prayer.

➤ Put a squiggle line under how Hannah thanked God.

Prayer Prompts:

➤ Praise God for an answered prayer.

➤ Confess a lack of faith.

➤ Pray for something you have been praying about for a long time.

➤ Pray for something you need today.

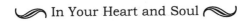 In Your Heart and Soul

Day 82: 1 Samuel 3:1 – 19

Bible Study:

➢ Double underline God's words.

➢ Circle Samuel's obedience.

➢ Highlight a passage that speaks to you.

➢ What thought did God give to you while reading this passage?

_____

_____

_____

Prayer Prompts:

➢ Praise God for speaking to you.

➢ Confess ignoring God's calling.

➢ Pray that you will hear His voice.

➢ Pray for the needs of someone else.

➢ Pray for something you need today.

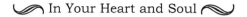

Day 83: 1 Samuel 4:1 – 11

Bible Study:

➢ Underline and define words you do not know.

_____

_____

_____

_____

➢ Put an exclamation point (!) next to the sins.

➢ Box the people's response.

➢ Double underline God's words.

➢ Put an X next to Samuel's response.

➢ What thought did God give to you while reading this passage?

_____

_____

_____

_____

Prayer Prompts:

➢ Praise God for something He has given to you.

➢ Confess taking that thing for granted.

➢ Pray for a thankful spirit.

➢ Pray for the needs of someone else.

➢ Pray for something you need today.

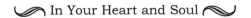

Day 84: 1 Samuel 5:1 – 12

Bible Study:

➢ Underline and define words you do not know.

_____

_____

_____

➢ Put an exclamation point (!) next to what the Philistine's did.

➢ Put an X next to what happened because of the Philistine's actions.

➢ What thought did God give to you while reading this passage?

_____

_____

_____

Prayer Prompts:

➢ Praise God for His mighty power.

➢ Confess a sin you committed today.

➢ Pray for your enemies.

➢ Pray for the needs of someone else.

➢ Pray for something you need today.

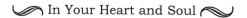

Day 85: 1 Samuel 8:1 – 22

Bible Study:

➤ Underline and define words you do not know.

_____

_____

_____

➤ Put an exclamation point (!) next to the sins.

➤ Box the people's request.

➤ Double underline God's words.

➤ Put an X next to Samuel's response.

➤ What thought did God give to you while reading this passage?

_____

_____

_____

Prayer Prompts:

➤ Praise God for answered prayers.

➤ Confess asking for the wrong things.

➤ Pray for wisdom.

➤ Pray for the needs of someone else.

➤ Pray for something you need today.

Day 86: 1 Samuel 9:1 – 17 & 10:1

Bible Study:

➤ Underline and define words you do not know.

_____

_____

_____

➤ Circle Saul's description.

➤ Double underline God's words.

➤ Highlight a passage that speaks to you.

Prayer Prompts:

➤ Praise God for His plans for you.

➤ Confess any desires that contrast with God's plans for you.

➤ Pray for grace.

➤ Pray for the needs of someone else.

➤ Pray for something you need today.

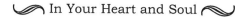

Day 87: 1 Samuel 13:1 – 14

Bible Study:

➤ Underline and define words you do not know.

_____

_____

_____

➤ Put an exclamation point (!) next to Saul's sin.

➤ What was Saul's excuse?

_____

_____

➤ Put an X next to Saul's consequence.

Prayer Prompts:

➤ Praise God for a godly guidance counselor.

➤ Confess a sin you committed out of fear.

➤ Pray for courage.

➤ Pray for the needs of someone else.

➤ Pray for something you need today.

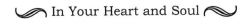 In Your Heart and Soul

Day 88: 1 Samuel 14:1 – 23

Bible Study:

➢ Underline and define words you do not know.

_____

_____

_____

➢ Put a box around Jonathan's actions.

➢ Highlight a passage that speaks to you.

➢ Write a thought God gave to you.

_____

_____

_____

Prayer Prompts:

➢ Praise God for protecting your country.

➢ Confess fear.

➢ Pray for courage to stand up for what is right.

➢ Pray for the needs of someone else.

➢ Pray for something you need today.

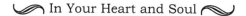

Day 89: 1 Samuel 15:10 – 23

Bible Study:

➤ Underline and define words you do not know.

_____

_____

_____

➤ Why was Saul's line removed from being king?

_____

_____

_____

➤ Highlight a passage that speaks to you.

➤ Write a thought God gave to you.

_____

_____

_____

Prayer Prompts:

➤ Praise God for being the controller of the world.

➤ Confess your sins from today.

➤ Pray for God to guide your ways.

➤ Pray for the needs of someone else.

➤ Pray for something you need today.

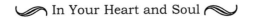

Day 90: 1 Samuel 16:1 – 13

Bible Study:

➢ Underline and define words you do not know.

_____

_____

_____

➢ Double underline God's words.

➢ Highlight verse 7.

➢ Write a thought God gave to you.

_____

_____

_____

Prayer Prompts:

➢ Praise God for His power on your life.

➢ Confess judging people by their appearances.

➢ Pray for God to see the goodness in your heart.

➢ Pray for the needs of someone else.

➢ Pray for something you need today.

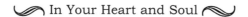

Day 91: Psalm 23:1 – 6

Bible Study:

➢ How does this Psalm reflect the heart of David?

_____

_____

_____

➢ Rewrite this psalm in your own words with your own life in mind.

_____

_____

_____

_____

_____

_____

_____

_____

_____

_____

_____

➢ Highlight a passage that speaks to you.

➢ Write a thought God gave to you.

_____

_____

_____

Prayer Prompts:

➢ Praise God for being your Shepherd.

➢ Confess taking your Shepherd for granted.

➢ Pray for the Psalm you rewrote to God.

➢ Pray for the needs of someone else.

➢ Pray for something you need today.

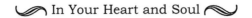

Day 92: 1 Samuel 17:1 – 52

Bible Study:

➢ Look up a map of this location.

➢ How tall was Goliath? _____

➢ Put an exclamation point (!) next to what Goliath said.

➢ Circle David's faith.

➢ Put two stars next to the miracle.

➢ Put an X next to what happened to Goliath.

Prayer Prompts:

➢ Praise God for defeating your enemies.

➢ Confess doubting God's power.

➢ Pray for God to give you courage when facing your enemies.

➢ Pray for the needs of someone else.

➢ Pray for something you need today.

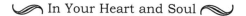

Day 93: 1 Samuel 18:1 – 14

Bible Study:

➢ Underline and define words you do not know.

_____

_____

_____

➢ Put an exclamation point (!) next to what Saul's sin.

➢ Star David's actions.

➢ Write a thought God gave to you.

_____

_____

_____

Prayer Prompts:

➢ Praise God for your friends.

➢ Confess jealousy.

➢ Pray for your friends.

➢ Pray for the needs of someone else.

➢ Pray for something you need today.

Day 94: 1 Samuel 19:9 – 10, 20:4 – 13, 35 – 39

Bible Study:

➤ Put an exclamation point (!) next to what Saul's sin.

➤ What was David and Jonathan's plan?

_____

_____

_____

➤ Why did David have to flee?

_____

_____

_____

➤ Write a thought God gave to you.

_____

_____

_____

Prayer Prompts:

➤ Praise God for your best friend.

➤ Confess anger.

➤ Pray for your best friend.

➤ Pray for the needs of someone else.

➤ Pray for something you need today.

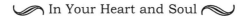

Day 95: Psalm 18:1 – 50

Bible Study:

➢ Put a squiggle line under what David calls God.

➢ How did David express his feelings?

_____

_____

_____

➢ Highlight a passage that speaks to you.

➢ Write a thought God gave to you.

_____

_____

_____

Prayer Prompts:

➢ Praise God for hearing your cries.

➢ Confess keeping your feelings from God.

➢ Pray about the feelings you are experiencing right now.

➢ Pray for the needs of someone else.

➢ Pray for something you need today.

Day 96: 1 Samuel 24:1 – 22

Bible Study:

➤ Put boxes around both Saul and David's actions.

➤ What was David's resolution?

_____

_____

_____

➤ What was Saul's resolution?

_____

_____

_____

➤ Highlight a passage that speaks to you.

➤ Write a thought God gave to you.

_____

_____

_____

Prayer Prompts:

➤ Praise God for His protection.

➤ Confess anger towards God's anointed.

➤ Pray for the leaders in your life.

➤ Pray for the needs of someone else.

➤ Pray for something you need today.

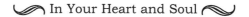

Day 97: Psalms 142:1 – 7 & 57:1-11

Bible Study:

➤ Put a squiggle line under what David said to God.

➤ How did David feel at the beginning of each Psalm?

_____

_____

_____

➤ How did David feel at the end of each Psalm?

_____

_____

_____

➤ Highlight a passage that speaks to you.

➤ Write a thought God gave to you.

_____

_____

_____

Prayer Prompts:

➤ Praise God for hearing your cries.

➤ Confess keeping your cares to yourself.

➤ Pray for God to take your cares away.

➤ Pray for the needs of someone else.

➤ Pray for something you need today.

Day 98: 1 Chronicles 10:1 – 14

Bible Study:

➢ Box what happened to Jonathan and Saul.

➢ Put an exclamation point (!) next to what Saul did wrong.

➢ Put an X next to Saul's consequences.

➢ Highlight a passage that speaks to you.

➢ Write a thought God gave to you.

_____

_____

_____

Prayer Prompts:

➢ Praise God for His justice.

➢ Confess going against God's wishes.

➢ Pray that you will honor God with your actions.

➢ Pray for the needs of someone else.

➢ Pray for something you need today.

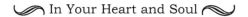

Day 99: 2 Samuel 2:1 – 7

Bible Study:

➢   What did David do first?

_____

_____

➢   Double underline God's words.

➢   Circle David's obedience.

➢   Put an arrow next to the act of kindness.

➢   Highlight a passage that speaks to you.

➢   Write a thought God gave to you.

_____

_____

_____

Prayer Prompts:

➢   Praise God for His kindness to you.

➢   Confess wishing ill to those that have hurt you.

➢   Pray for God to give you someone to be kind to.

➢   Pray for the needs of someone else.

➢   Pray for something you need today.

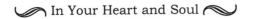

Day 100: 2 Samuel 6:1 – 21

Bible Study:

➤ Put an exclamation point (!) next to what Uzzah did.

➤ Put an X next to what happened to Uzzah.

➤ How did David react to what happened to Uzzah?

_____

_____

_____

➤ What changed David's mind?

_____

_____

_____

➤ Put a squiggle line under how David praised God.

➤ Put an exclamation point (!) next to what Michal did.

➤ What was David's answer to Michal?

_____

_____

_____

➤ Highlight a passage that speaks to you.

➤ Write a thought God gave to you.

_____

_____

_____

Prayer Prompts:

➤ Praise God for His justness.

➤ Confess your frustrations with the Christian life.

➤ Pray for understanding when you are frustrated.

➤ Pray for the needs of someone else.

➤ Pray for something you need today.

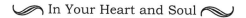

Day 101: 1 Chronicles 17:1 – 27

Bible Study:

➢ Underline and define words you do not know.

_____

_____

_____

➢ Put a squiggle line under David's desire.

➢ Double underline God's words.

➢ What was David's response to God's answer?

_____

_____

_____

➢ Put a squiggle line under how David praised God.

➢ How do you handle being told, "no," by God?

_____

_____

_____

➢ Highlight a passage that speaks to you.

➢ Write a thought God gave to you.

_____

_____

_____

Prayer Prompts:

➢ Praise God for His will for your life.

➢ Confess desiring your will over God's will.

➢ Pray for God to show you His will for your life.

➢ Pray for the needs of someone else.

➢ Pray for something you need today.

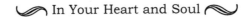

Day 102: 2 Samuel 9:1 – 13

Bible Study:

➢ Underline and define words you do not know.

_____

_____

_____

➢ Put an arrow next to the kind act.

➢ Why did David show Mephibosheth kindness?

_____

_____

_____

➢ Who is someone you can show kindness to because someone else was kind to you?

_____

_____

_____

➢ Highlight a passage that speaks to you.

➢ Write a thought God gave to you.

_____

_____

_____

Prayer Prompts:

➢ Praise God for the kindness of others.

➢ Confess forgetting to be kind to others.

➢ Pray for someone who needs kindness shown to them.

➢ Pray for the needs of someone else.

➢ Pray for something you need today.

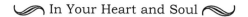

Day 103: 2 Samuel 23:8 – 22

Bible Study:

- ➤ Put an arrow next to what the mighty men did for David.

- ➤ Put a squiggle line under how David worshipped God.

- ➤ List the mighty men and their accomplishments:

_____

_____

_____

_____

_____

_____

_____

_____

- ➤ Highlight a passage that speaks to you.

- ➤ Write a thought God gave to you.

_____

_____

_____

Prayer Prompts:

- ➤ Praise God for a kindness shown to you.

- ➤ Confess ignoring the leading of God.

- ➤ Pray for God to give you someone to be kind to.

- ➤ Pray for the needs of someone else.

- ➤ Pray for something you need today.

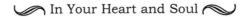

Day 104: 1 Chronicles 29:1 – 25

Bible Study:

➤ Underline and define words you do not know.

_____

_____

_____

➤ Put a squiggle line under how David worshipped God.

➤ Put a squiggle line under all David gave to God's house.

➤ What was David's spirit while giving?

_____

_____

➤ What can you give to God's house?

_____

_____

_____

➤ Highlight a passage that speaks to you.

➤ Write a thought God gave to you.

_____

_____

_____

Prayer Prompts:

➤ Praise God for giving you a place to worship.

➤ Confess holding things back from God.

➤ Pray for God to give you a willing heart.

➤ Pray for the needs of someone else.

➤ Pray for something you need today.

Day 105: Psalm 14:1 – 7

Bible Study:

➤ Underline and define words you do not know.

_____

_____

_____

➤ Put an exclamation point (!) next to what the fool does.

➤ Write what David is saying in your own words.

_____

_____

_____

_____

_____

_____

_____

_____

_____

_____

➤ Highlight a passage that speaks to you.

➤ Write a thought God gave to you.

_____

_____

_____

Prayer Prompts:

➤ Praise God for being our refuge.

➤ Confess foolish thoughts.

➤ Pray for a clean heart before God.

➤ Pray for the needs of someone else.

➤ Pray for something you need today.

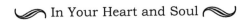

Day 106: Psalm 19:1 – 14

Bible Study:

➢ Underline and define words you do not know.

_____

_____

_____

➢ Who is speaking? _____

➢ To whom is he speaking? _____

➢ Highlight a passage that speaks to you.

➢ Write a thought God gave to you.

_____

_____

_____

➢ Memorize verses 7 – 11. (It is a song.) or Memorize verse 14. (Another song.)

Prayer Prompts:

➢ Praise God for the sky declaring God's glory.

➢ Confess ignoring God's handiwork.

➢ Pray for a praising spirit.

➢ Pray for the needs of someone else.

➢ Pray for something you need today.

Day 107: Psalm 24:1 – 10

Bible Study:

➢ Underline and define words you do not know.

_____

_____

_____

➢ Put a squiggle line under the praises.

➢ Highlight a passage that speaks to you.

➢ Write a thought God gave to you.

_____

_____

_____

Prayer Prompts:

➢ Praise God as the Lord of the earth.

➢ Confess a sin you committed today.

➢ Pray for the earth.

➢ Pray for the needs of someone else.

➢ Pray for something you need today.

Day 108: Psalm 25:1 – 22

Bible Study:

➢ Put a squiggle line under the praises.

➢ What was David asking for?

➢ Highlight a passage that speaks to you.

➢ Write a thought God gave to you.

_____

_____

_____

➢ Memorize verses 1 – 4. (It is a song.)

Prayer Prompts:

➢ Praise God for hearing you.

➢ Confess being ashamed of God.

➢ Pray for boldness.

➢ Pray for the needs of someone else.

➢ Pray for something you need today.

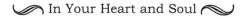

Day 109: Psalm 27:1 – 14

Bible Study:

➤ Underline and define words you do not know.

_____

_____

_____

➤ Put a squiggle line under the praises.

➤ Highlight a passage that speaks to you.

➤ Write a thought God gave to you.

_____

_____

_____

➤ Memorize verse 14.

Prayer Prompts:

➤ Praise God for being your strength.

➤ Confess not waiting on the Lord.

➤ Pray for deliverance from your enemies.

➤ Pray for the needs of someone else.

➤ Pray for something you need today.

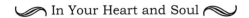

Day 110: Psalm 46:1 – 11

Bible Study:

➢ Underline and define words you do not know.

_____

_____

_____

➢ Rewrite this Psalm in your own words.

_____

_____

_____

_____

_____

_____

_____

_____

_____

_____

_____

➢ Highlight a passage that speaks to you.

➢ Write a thought God gave to you.

_____

_____

_____

➢ Memorize verse 10.

Prayer Prompts:

➢ Praise God for being your refuge.

➢ Confess your fears.

➢ Pray for God to be exalted on the earth.

➢ Pray for the needs of someone else.

➢ Pray for something you need today.

/4

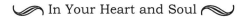

Day 111: Psalm 47:1 – 9

Bible Study:

➢ Underline and define words you do not know.

_____

_____

_____

➢ Put a squiggle line under the praises.

➢ Highlight a passage that speaks to you.

➢ Write a thought God gave to you.

_____

_____

_____

➢ Memorize verse 1.

Prayer Prompts:

➢ Praise God using a verse from the psalm.

➢ Confess your sins from today.

➢ Pray for God to give you a praising spirit.

➢ Pray for the needs of someone else.

➢ Pray for something you need today.

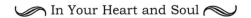

Day 112: Psalm 48:1 – 14

Bible Study:

➤ Underline and define words you do not know.

_____

_____

_____

➤ Put a squiggle line under the praises.

➤ Highlight a passage that speaks to you.

➤ Write a thought God gave to you.

_____

_____

_____

➤ Memorize verses 1 - 2.

Prayer Prompts:

➤ Praise God as the joy of the earth.

➤ Confess fear.

➤ Pray for God to be your guide.

➤ Pray for the needs of someone else.

➤ Pray for something you need today.

Day 113: Psalm 121:1 – 8

Bible Study:

➤ Put a squiggle line under the praises.

➤ Rewrite this Psalm in your own words.

_____

_____

_____

_____

_____

_____

_____

_____

_____

_____

_____

_____

_____

_____

➤ Highlight a passage that speaks to you.

➤ Write a thought God gave to you.

_____

_____

_____

➤ Memorize verses 1 - 8. (It is a song.)

Prayer Prompts:

➤ Praise God for being your help.

➤ Confess looking for help elsewhere.

➤ Pray for God to preserve you from all evil.

➤ Pray for the needs of someone else.

➤ Pray for something you need today.

Day 114: 2 Chronicles 1:1 – 17

Bible Study:

- ➤ Put a squiggle line under how Solomon worshipped.
- ➤ Double underline God's words.
- ➤ Put a star next to Solomon's wise request.
- ➤ Put an arrow next to how Solomon was blessed.
- ➤ What would you have asked for?

_____

_____

_____

- ➤ Highlight a passage that speaks to you.
- ➤ Write a thought God gave to you.

_____

_____

_____

Prayer Prompts:

- ➤ Praise God for His gifts to you.
- ➤ Confess asking for the wrong things.
- ➤ Pray for wisdom.
- ➤ Pray for the needs of someone else.
- ➤ Pray for something you need today.

Day 115: 1 Kings 3:16 – 28

Bible Study:

➤ Underline and define words you do not know.

_____

_____

_____

➤ What was the claim of the two women?

_____

_____

_____

➤ Put a star next to Solomon's response.

➤ Why was this a wise response?

_____

_____

_____

➤ How would you have judged these women?

_____

_____

_____

_____

➤ Highlight a passage that speaks to you.

➤ Write a thought God gave to you.

_____

_____

_____

Prayer Prompts:

➤ Praise God for wisdom in difficult situations.

➤ Confess acting without wisdom.

➤ Pray for wisdom in your actions.

➤ Pray for the needs of someone else.

➤ Pray for something you need today.

Day 116: 2 Chronicles 3:1 – 17

Bible Study:

➤ Draw a picture of the tabernacle from the description in the passage:

➤ Highlight a passage that speaks to you.

➤ Write a thought God gave to you.

_____

_____

_____

Prayer Prompts:

➤ Praise God for your church.

➤ Confess having any bad feelings about your church.

➤ Pray for your church, its ministries, and its members.

➤ Pray for the needs of someone else.

➤ Pray for something you need today.

Day 117: Proverbs 1:1 – 19

Bible Study:

- ➤ Who is speaking?
- ➤ To whom is he speaking?
- ➤ Put stars next to the instructions.
- ➤ Put an exclamation point (!) next to what the fools and sinners do.
- ➤ Put an X next to what happens to them.
- ➤ Highlight a passage that speaks to you.
- ➤ Write a thought God gave to you.

_____

_____

_____

Prayer Prompts:

- ➤ Praise God for your father.
- ➤ Confess listening to fools.
- ➤ Pray for wisdom with friends.
- ➤ Pray for the needs of someone else.
- ➤ Pray for something you need today.

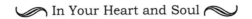

Day 118: Proverbs 3:1 – 35

Bible Study:

➢ Put stars next to the instructions.

➢ Highlight a passage that speaks to you.

➢ Write a thought God gave to you.

_____

_____

_____

➢ Memorize verses 5 – 7.

Prayer Prompts:

➢ Praise God for instruction.

➢ Confess acting without wisdom.

➢ Pray for a trait from this passage that you would like to develop.

➢ Pray for the needs of someone else.

➢ Pray for something you need today.

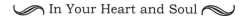

Day 119: Proverbs 11:1 – 31

Bible Study:

➢ Who is speaking?

➢ To whom is he speaking?

➢ Put stars next to the instructions.

➢ Highlight a passage that speaks to you.

➢ Write a thought God gave to you.

_____

_____

_____

Prayer Prompts:

➢ Praise God for the Bible.

➢ Confess a sin you committed today.

➢ Pray for wisdom in your actions.

➢ Pray for the needs of someone else.

➢ Pray for something you need today.

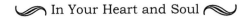

Day 120: Proverbs 14:1 – 35

Bible Study:

➢ Put stars next to the instructions.

➢ Circle the instructions you need to work on.

➢ Highlight a passage that speaks to you.

➢ Write a thought God gave to you.

_____

_____

_____

Prayer Prompts:

➢ Praise God for changing your life.

➢ Confess the instructions you are not following.

➢ Pray for the instructions you need to work on.

➢ Pray for the needs of someone else.

➢ Pray for something you need today.

Day 121: Proverbs 20:1 – 30

Bible Study:

➢ Put stars next to the instructions.

➢ Circle the instructions you need to work on.

➢ Highlight a passage that speaks to you.

➢ Write a thought God gave to you.

_____

_____

_____

Prayer Prompts:

➢ Praise God for speaking to you.

➢ Confess the instructions you are not following.

➢ Pray for the instructions you need to work on.

➢ Pray for the needs of someone else.

➢ Pray for something you need today.

Day 122: Proverbs 22:1 – 29

Bible Study:

➢ Put stars next to the instructions.

➢ Circle the instructions you need to work on.

➢ Highlight a passage that speaks to you.

➢ Write a thought God gave to you.

_____

_____

_____

➢ Memorize verse 1.

Prayer Prompts:

➢ Praise God using His names in the Bible.

➢ Confess the instructions you are not following.

➢ Pray for the instructions you need to work on.

➢ Pray for the needs of someone else.

➢ Pray for something you need today.

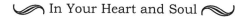

Day 123: Proverbs 31:10 – 31

Bible Study:

➤ Put stars next to the wise attributes.

➤ List things the virtuous woman does:

_____

_____

_____

_____

_____

_____

_____

_____

_____

_____

_____

_____

_____

_____

➤ Highlight a passage that speaks to you.

➤ Write a thought God gave to you.

_____

_____

_____

Prayer Prompts:

➤ Praise God for a godly woman in your life.

➤ Confess any issues with your mother.

➤ Pray for godly women in your life.

➤ Pray for the needs of someone else.

➤ Pray for something you need today.

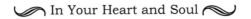

Day 124: Ecclesiastes 1:1 – 18

Bible Study:

➤ Who is speaking? _____

➤ What is he speaking about?

_____

_____

_____

➤ Highlight a passage that speaks to you.

➤ Write a thought God gave to you.

_____

_____

_____

Prayer Prompts:

➤ Praise God for the earth.

➤ Confess vanities in your life.

➤ Pray for understanding.

➤ Pray for the needs of someone else.

➤ Pray for something you need today.

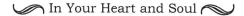

Day 125: Ecclesiastes 3:1 – 22

Bible Study:

➤ Underline and define words you do not know.

_____

_____

_____

➤ List the different times of your life:

_____

_____

_____

_____

_____

_____

_____

_____

_____

_____

_____

➤ Highlight a passage that speaks to you.

➤ Write a thought God gave to you.

_____

_____

_____

➤ Memorize verse 11.

Prayer Prompts:

➤ Praise God for the season you are in.

➤ Confess anger toward the season you are in.

➤ Pray for you to enjoy the season you are in.

➤ Pray for the needs of someone else.

➤ Pray for something you need today.

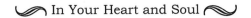

Day 126: Ecclesiastes 12:1 – 14

Bible Study:

➢ Underline and define words you do not know.

_____

_____

_____

➢ Put stars next to the instructions.

➢ Highlight a passage that speaks to you.

➢ Write a thought God gave to you.

_____

_____

_____

Prayer Prompts:

➢ Praise God for being your creator.

➢ Confess not keeping God's commandments.

➢ Pray for help you with keeping the commandments.

➢ Pray for the needs of someone else.

➢ Pray for something you need today.

Day 127: 1 Kings 12:1 – 19

Bible Study:

➢ Underline and define words you do not know.

_____

_____

_____

➢ Put an exclamation point (!) next to the bad advice.

➢ Put an X next to what happened to Israel.

➢ Highlight a passage that speaks to you.

➢ Write a thought God gave to you.

_____

_____

_____

Prayer Prompts:

➢ Praise God for those in authority over you.

➢ Confess ignoring good advice.

➢ Pray for those in authority over you.

➢ Pray for the needs of someone else.

➢ Pray for something you need today.

Day 128: 1 Kings 16:29 – 33

Bible Study:

➢ Underline and define words you do not know.

_____

_____

_____

➢ Put an exclamation point (!) next to Ahab's actions.

➢ Highlight a passage that speaks to you.

➢ Write a thought God gave to you.

_____

_____

_____

Prayer Prompts:

➢ Praise God for His just nature.

➢ Confess doing something you know was wrong.

➢ Confess sins you committed today.

➢ Pray that you do not provoke God's anger.

➢ Pray for the needs of someone else.

➢ Pray for something you need today.

Day 129: 1 Kings 17:1 – 7

Bible Study:

➢ Underline and define words you do not know.

_____

_____

_____

➢ Double underline God's words.

➢ Circle Elijah's obedience.

➢ Double star the miracles.

➢ Highlight a passage that speaks to you.

➢ Write a thought God gave to you.

_____

_____

_____

Prayer Prompts:

➢ Praise God for taking care of you each day.

➢ Confess disobedience.

➢ Confess sins you committed today.

➢ Rain is often a symbol of blessings. Pray for rain and blessing for your country.

➢ Pray for the needs of someone else.

➢ Pray for something you need today.

Day 130: 1 Kings 17:8 – 24

Bible Study:

➢ Double underline God's words.

➢ Circle the acts of obedience.

➢ What was the widow's problem?

_____

_____

_____

➢ Double star the miracles.

➢ Highlight a passage that speaks to you.

➢ Write a thought God gave to you.

_____

_____

_____

Prayer Prompts:

➢ Praise God for a miracle in your life.

➢ Confess fear and stress about your needs.

➢ Confess sins you committed today.

➢ Pray for someone who is sick.

➢ Pray for the needs of someone else.

➢ Pray for something you need today.

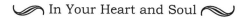

Day 131: 1 Kings 18:17 – 29

Bible Study:

➤ Underline and define words you do not know.

_____

_____

_____

➤ What was the test?

_____

_____

_____

➤ Put an exclamation point (!) next to how the people worshiped Baal.

➤ Highlight a passage that speaks to you.

➤ Write a thought God gave to you.

_____

_____

_____

Prayer Prompts:

➤ Praise God for the one true God.

➤ Confess anything that comes before God in your life.

➤ Confess sins you committed today.

➤ Pray for God to be exalted.

➤ Pray for the needs of someone else.

➤ Pray for something you need today.

Day 132: 1 Kings 18:30 – 40

Bible Study:

➢   Underline and define words you do not know.

_____

_____

_____

➢   How did Elijah prepare his alter?

_____

_____

_____

➢   Put a squiggle line under Elijah's prayer.

➢   Double star the miracle.

➢   Highlight a passage that speaks to you.

➢   Write a thought God gave to you.

_____

_____

_____

Prayer Prompts:

➢   Praise God answered prayers.

➢   Confess doubting God's power.

➢   Confess sins you committed today.

➢   Pray for your country to turn to God.

➢   Pray for the needs of someone else.

➢   Pray for something you need today.

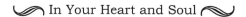

Day 133: 1 Kings 18:41 – 46

Bible Study:

➢ What did Elijah prophecy about?

_____

_____

_____

➢ Did God answer Elijah's prayer right away?

_____

_____

_____

➢ Should you stop praying if God does not answer right away?

_____

_____

_____

➢ Double star the answered prayer.

➢ Highlight a passage that speaks to you.

➢ Write a thought God gave to you.

_____

_____

_____

Prayer Prompts:

➢ Praise God rain.

➢ Confess giving up on prayer.

➢ Confess sins you committed today.

➢ Pray for unanswered prayers.

➢ Pray for the needs of someone else.

➢ Pray for something you need today.

Day 134: 1 Kings 19:1 – 8

Bible Study:

➤ Put an exclamation point (!) next to what Jezebel did.

➤ Where did Elijah run to?

_____

_____

_____

➤ How did Elijah feel?

_____

_____

_____

➤ Double star how God took care of Elijah.

➤ Highlight a passage that speaks to you.

➤ Write a thought God gave to you.

_____

_____

_____

Prayer Prompts:

➤ Praise God for daily provisions.

➤ Confess discouragement.

➤ Confess sins you committed today.

➤ Pray for encouragement from God.

➤ Pray for the needs of someone else.

➤ Pray for something you need today.

Day 135: 1 Kings 19:9 – 21

Bible Study:

➤ Double underline God's words.

➤ How was Elijah feeling?

_____

_____

_____

➤ Double star the miracles.

➤ What was God in?

_____

_____

_____

➤ Highlight a passage that speaks to you.

➤ Write a thought God gave to you.

_____

_____

_____

Prayer Prompts:

➤ Praise God for His understanding.

➤ Confess jealousy.

➤ Confess sins you committed today.

➤ Pray for someone that needs encouragement.

➤ Pray for the needs of someone else.

➤ Pray for something you need today.

Day 136: 1 Kings 21:1 – 29

Bible Study:

➢ What did Ahab want?

_____

_____

_____

➢ Why wouldn't Naboth give it to him?

_____

_____

_____

➢ Put an exclamation point (!) next to Ahab's reaction.

➢ Put an exclamation point (!) next to what Jezebel did.

➢ Double underline God's words.

➢ Put an X next to what will happen to Ahab and Jezebel.

➢ Circle Ahab's repentance.

➢ Highlight a passage that speaks to you.

➢ Write a thought God gave to you.

_____

_____

_____

Prayer Prompts:

➢ Praise God for His vengeance.

➢ Confess coveting someone else's things.

➢ Confess sins you committed today.

➢ Pray for a content spirit.

➢ Pray for the needs of someone else.

➢ Pray for something you need today.

Day 137: 2 Kings 2:1 – 14

Bible Study:

➤ Double star the miracles.

➤ Why do you think Elijah wanted Elisha to stay behind?

_____

_____

_____

➤ Why wouldn't Elisha stay behind?

_____

_____

_____

➤ Circle Elisha's faith.

➤ Highlight a passage that speaks to you.

➤ Write a thought God gave to you.

_____

_____

_____

Prayer Prompts:

➤ Praise God for His power in your life.

➤ Confess giving up.

➤ Confess sins you committed today.

➤ Pray for strength of character.

➤ Pray for the needs of someone else.

➤ Pray for something you need today.

Day 138: 2 Kings 4:1 – 7

Bible Study:

➢ Underline and define words you do not know.

_____

_____

_____

➢ Double star the miracles.

➢ Circle the widow's obedience.

➢ Highlight a passage that speaks to you.

➢ Write a thought God gave to you.

_____

_____

_____

Prayer Prompts:

➢ Praise God for taking care of you.

➢ Confess acting out of fear.

➢ Confess sins you committed today.

➢ Pray for money for your bills.

➢ Pray for the needs of someone else.

➢ Pray for something you need today.

Day 139: 2 Kings 4:8 – 17

Bible Study:

➤ Put an arrow next to the woman's kindness.

➤ Put an arrow next to how Elisha wanted to thank her.

➤ Double star the miracle.

➤ Highlight a passage that speaks to you.

➤ Write a thought God gave to you.

_____

_____

_____

Prayer Prompts:

➤ Praise God for someone who has met your needs.

➤ Confess selfishness.

➤ Confess sins you committed today.

➤ Pray for someone that needs something.

➤ Pray for the needs of someone else.

➤ Pray for something you need today.

Decision:

➤ How can you meet a need in someone's life?

_____

_____

_____

Day 140: 2 Kings 4:18 – 37

Bible Study:

➢ What happened to the boy?

_____

_____

_____

➢ What was the mother's response?

_____

_____

_____

➢ Double star the miracle.

➢ Highlight a passage that speaks to you.

➢ Write a thought God gave to you.

_____

_____

_____

Prayer Prompts:

➢ Praise God for someone that was healed.

➢ Confess anger about sickness and death.

➢ Confess sins you committed today.

➢ Pray for someone that has suffered a loss.

➢ Pray for the needs of someone else.

➢ Pray for something you need today.

Day 141: 2 Kings 5:1 – 14

Bible Study:

➢ Underline and define words you do not know.

_____

_____

_____

➢ Put an arrow next to the maid's kindness.

➢ Put an exclamation point (!) next to Naaman's reaction.

➢ Circle Naaman's obedience.

➢ Double star the miracle.

➢ Highlight a passage that speaks to you.

➢ Write a thought God gave to you.

_____

_____

_____

Prayer Prompts:

➢ Praise God for kind people.

➢ Confess a bad attitude.

➢ Confess sins you committed today.

➢ Pray for healing.

➢ Pray for the needs of someone else.

➢ Pray for something you need today.

Day 142: Isaiah 1:1, 6:1, & 6:8 – 12

Bible Study:

➢ Underline and define words you do not know.

_____

_____

_____

➢ Circle Isaiah's response.

➢ What is going to happen?

_____

_____

_____

➢ Highlight a passage that speaks to you.

➢ Write a thought God gave to you.

_____

_____

_____

Prayer Prompts:

➢ Praise God for being all-knowing.

➢ Confess not understanding God's will.

➢ Confess sins you committed today.

➢ Pray for understanding.

➢ Pray for the needs of someone else.

➢ Pray for something you need today.

Day 143: 2 Kings 6:8 – 18

Bible Study:

- ➤ Put an exclamation point (!) next to what the king of Israel did.
- ➤ Put a squiggle line under Elisha's prayer.
- ➤ Double star the miracle.
- ➤ How was God protecting Elisha?

_____

_____

_____

- ➤ Highlight a passage that speaks to you.
- ➤ Write a thought God gave to you.

_____

_____

_____

Prayer Prompts:

- ➤ Praise God for angel's protecting you.
- ➤ Confess unbelief.
- ➤ Confess sins you committed today.
- ➤ Pray for angels to protect your loved ones.
- ➤ Pray for the needs of someone else.
- ➤ Pray for something you need today.

Day 144: 2 Kings 11:1 – 12

Bible Study:

➢ Put an arrow next to the act of mercy.

➢ Box how the people protected Joash.

➢ Circle the captain's obedience.

➢ Highlight a passage that speaks to you.

➢ Write a thought God gave to you.

_____

_____

_____

Prayer Prompts:

➢ Praise God for the people that protect you.

➢ Confess not helping others.

➢ Confess sins you committed today.

➢ Pray for someone that needs your protection.

➢ Pray for the needs of someone else.

➢ Pray for something you need today.

Day 145: 2 Kings 11:17 – 21

Bible Study:

➤ Put an arrow next to Jehoiada's covenant.

➤ Circle what the people did to the house of Baal.

➤ How old was the king at the start of his reign? _____

➤ Highlight a passage that speaks to you.

➤ Write a thought God gave to you.

_____

_____

_____

Prayer Prompts:

➤ Praise God for people that turn back to God.

➤ Confess stubbornness.

➤ Confess sins you committed today.

➤ Pray for your country to have revival.

➤ Pray for the needs of someone else.

➤ Pray for something you need today.

Day 146: 2 Kings 12:1 – 14

Bible Study:

- ➤ Circle how Joash reigned.
- ➤ Put an exclamation point (!) next to what the priests did not do.
- ➤ Put an arrow next to how the people reacted.
- ➤ Highlight a passage that speaks to you.
- ➤ Write a thought God gave to you.

_____

_____

_____

Prayer Prompts:

- ➤ Praise God for your church.
- ➤ Confess holding your money and talents back from the church.
- ➤ Confess sins you committed today.
- ➤ Pray for something at church to give money to.
- ➤ Pray for the needs of someone else.
- ➤ Pray for something you need today.

Day 147: 2 Kings 13:20 – 21

Bible Study:

➢   Underline and define words you do not know.

_____

_____

_____

➢   Double star the miracle.

➢   Highlight a passage that speaks to you.

➢   Write a thought God gave to you.

_____

_____

_____

Prayer Prompts:

➢   Praise God for the miracles in your life.

➢   Confess a lack of faith.

➢   Confess sins you committed today.

➢   Pray for God to use you.

➢   Pray for the needs of someone else.

➢   Pray for something you need today.

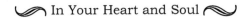

Day 148: Jonah 1:1 – 17

Bible Study:

➢ Underline and define words you do not know.

_____

_____

_____

➢ Put an exclamation point (!) next to Jonah's disobedience.

➢ Put an X next to what happened to Jonah.

➢ Highlight a passage that speaks to you.

➢ Write a thought God gave to you.

_____

_____

_____

Prayer Prompts:

➢ Praise God for controlling the world.

➢ Confess disobeying God.

➢ Confess sins you committed today.

➢ Pray for God to show you His will for your life.

➢ Pray for the needs of someone else.

➢ Pray for something you need today.

Day 149: Jonah 2:1 – 3:10

Bible Study:

➢ Circle Jonah's repentance.

➢ Put a squiggle line under Jonah's prayer.

➢ Double underline God's words.

➢ Circle Jonah's obedience.

➢ Circle the people's repentance.

➢ Put an X next to God's response to their repentance.

➢ Highlight a passage that speaks to you.

➢ Write a thought God gave to you.

_____

_____

_____

Prayer Prompts:

➢ Praise God for second chances.

➢ Confess not obeying right away.

➢ Confess sins you committed today.

➢ Pray for God to give you another chance.

➢ Pray for the needs of someone else.

➢ Pray for something you need today.

Day 150: Jonah 4:1 – 11

Bible Study:

➤ Put an exclamation point (!) next to Jonah's anger.

➤ Put a squiggle line under Jonah's prayer.

➤ Double underline God's words.

➤ Circle Jonah's obedience.

➤ Double underline the miracles.

➤ What was Jonah's attitude and why?

_____

_____

_____

➤ Highlight a passage that speaks to you.

➤ Write a thought God gave to you.

_____

_____

_____

Prayer Prompts:

➤ Praise God for His grace and mercy.

➤ Confess a bad attitude.

➤ Confess sins you committed today.

➤ Pray for mercy when you are in a bad mood.

➤ Pray for the needs of someone else.

➤ Pray for something you need today.

Day 151: 2 Kings 18:1 – 12

Bible Study:

- ➤ Circle what Hezekiah did.
- ➤ Put a star next to verse 6.
- ➤ Put an X next to the Lord's response.
- ➤ Put an exclamation point (!) next to what Assyria did to Israel.
- ➤ Highlight a passage that speaks to you.
- ➤ Write a thought God gave to you.

_____

_____

_____

Prayer Prompts:

- ➤ Praise God for a blessing you have received.
- ➤ Confess doing wrong in the eyes of the Lord.
- ➤ Confess sins you committed today.
- ➤ Pray for the Lord to prosper you.
- ➤ Pray for the needs of someone else.
- ➤ Pray for something you need today.

Day 152: 2 Chronicles 32:1 – 8

Bible Study:

➢ Put a star next to how Hezekiah reacted to the Assyrians attacking them.

➢ Circle Hezekiah's faith.

➢ How do you react to being attacked?

_____

_____

_____

➢ Highlight a passage that speaks to you.

➢ Write a thought God gave to you.

_____

_____

_____

Prayer Prompts:

➢ Praise God for wise counselors in your life.

➢ Confess fear of your enemies.

➢ Confess sins you committed today.

➢ Pray for courage.

➢ Pray for the needs of someone else.

➢ Pray for something you need today.

Day 153: Isaiah 10:5 – 6, & 10:20 – 24

Bible Study:

- ➢ Who is speaking? _____
- ➢ To whom is he speaking? _____
- ➢ Double underline the prophecy.
- ➢ Highlight a passage that speaks to you.
- ➢ Write a thought God gave to you.

_____

_____

_____

Prayer Prompts:

- ➢ Praise God for delivering you from your enemies.
- ➢ Confess angering God.
- ➢ Confess sins you committed today.
- ➢ Pray for Israel.
- ➢ Pray for the needs of someone else.
- ➢ Pray for something you need today.

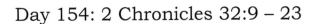

Day 154: 2 Chronicles 32:9 – 23

Bible Study:

➤ Put an exclamation point (!) next to what the Assyrian king said and did.

➤ Put a squiggle line under Hezekiah's prayer.

➤ Double underline how the Assyrian's were defeated.

➤ Put a squiggle line under how the people thanked God.

➤ Highlight a passage that speaks to you.

➤ Write a thought God gave to you.

_____

_____

_____

Prayer Prompts:

➤ Praise God for saving you.

➤ Confess trusting your own power rather than God's power.

➤ Confess sins you committed today.

➤ Pray for a miracle you would like to see.

➤ Pray for the needs of someone else.

➤ Pray for something you need today.

Day 155: 2 Kings 20:1 – 11

Bible Study:

- ➤ Double underline God's words.
- ➤ Put a squiggle line under Hezekiah's prayer.
- ➤ Put a double star next to the answered prayer.
- ➤ Put a squiggle line under Isaiah's prayer.
- ➤ Highlight a passage that speaks to you.
- ➤ Write a thought God gave to you.

_____

_____

_____

Prayer Prompts:

- ➤ Praise God for hearing our prayers.
- ➤ Confess not asking for the impossible.
- ➤ Confess sins you committed today.
- ➤ Pray for the faith to ask for miracles.
- ➤ Pray for the needs of someone else.
- ➤ Pray for something you need today.

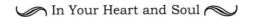

Day 156: 2 Kings 20:12 – 21

Bible Study:

➤ Put an exclamation point (!) next to what Hezekiah did.

➤ Double underline God's words.

➤ What was Hezekiah's reaction to the prophecy?

_____

_____

_____

➤ Highlight a passage that speaks to you.

➤ Write a thought God gave to you.

_____

_____

_____

Prayer Prompts:

➤ Praise God for the Bible.

➤ Confess apathy for future generations.

➤ Confess sins you committed today.

➤ Pray that you will be able to leave a legacy for the future.

➤ Pray for the needs of someone else.

➤ Pray for something you need today.

Day 157: Isaiah 40:1 & 26 – 31

Bible Study:

➤ Put a squiggle line under the names and descriptions of God.

➤ Double underline God's words.

➤ Highlight a passage that speaks to you.

➤ Write a thought God gave to you.

_____

_____

_____

➤ Memorize verse 31.

Prayer Prompts:

➤ Praise God for hearing your cry.

➤ Confess your weakness.

➤ Confess sins you committed today.

➤ Pray for comfort and strength.

➤ Pray for the needs of someone else.

➤ Pray for something you need today.

Day 158: 2 Kings 21:1 – 18

Bible Study:

- ➤ Put an exclamation point (!) next to the things Manasseh did.
- ➤ Double underline God's words.
- ➤ Why do you think Manasseh was so evil when he had a righteous father?

_____

_____

_____

- ➤ Highlight a passage that speaks to you.
- ➤ Write a thought God gave to you.

_____

_____

_____

Prayer Prompts:

- ➤ Praise God for His judgements.
- ➤ Confess forsaking your heritage.
- ➤ Confess sins you committed today.
- ➤ Pray for strength of character.
- ➤ Pray for the needs of someone else.
- ➤ Pray for something you need today.

Day 159: Nahum 1:1 – 15

Bible Study:

➢ Underline and define words you do not know.

_____

_____

_____

➢ Double underline God's words.

➢ Put a squiggle line under the descriptions of God.

➢ Highlight a passage that speaks to you.

➢ Write a thought God gave to you.

_____

_____

_____

Prayer Prompts:

➢ Praise God for His vengeance for you.

➢ Confess acts of revenge.

➢ Confess sins you committed today.

➢ Pray for God to defend and avenge you.

➢ Pray for the needs of someone else.

➢ Pray for something you need today.

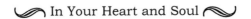

Day 160: 2 Chronicles 34:1 – 12

Bible Study:

➢ Underline and define words you do not know.

_____

_____

_____

➢ Circle what Josiah did.

➢ How do you do right in the eyes of the Lord.

_____

_____

_____

➢ Highlight a passage that speaks to you.

➢ Write a thought God gave to you.

_____

_____

_____

Prayer Prompts:

➢ Praise God for godly influences in your life.

➢ Confess listening to the wrong people.

➢ Confess sins you committed today.

➢ Pray for your godly leaders and friends.

➢ Pray for the needs of someone else.

➢ Pray for something you need today.

Day 161: 2 Kings 23:4 – 21

Bible Study:

➤ Underline and define words you do not know.

_____

_____

_____

➤ Circle what Josiah did.

➤ Is there an area in your life that needs to change?

_____

_____

_____

➤ Highlight a passage that speaks to you.

➤ Write a thought God gave to you.

_____

_____

_____

Prayer Prompts:

➤ Praise God for your church.

➤ Confess taking your Bible for granted.

➤ Confess sins you committed today.

➤ Pray for God to work mightily in your church.

➤ Pray for the needs of someone else.

➤ Pray for something you need today.

Day 162: Jeremiah 1:1 – 10

Bible Study:

➢ Double underline God's words.

➢ Put an exclamation point (!) next to Jeremiah's response.

➢ What words has God put in your mouth?

_____

_____

_____

➢ Highlight a passage that speaks to you.

➢ Write a thought God gave to you.

_____

_____

_____

Prayer Prompts:

➢ Praise God for having a plan for your life.

➢ Confess excuses you make for not serving God.

➢ Confess sins you committed today.

➢ Pray for courage and a willing heart.

➢ Pray for the needs of someone else.

➢ Pray for something you need today.

Day 163: Jeremiah 2:1 – 13

Bible Study:

➢ Double underline God's words.

➢ What sins has your country committed against God?

_____

_____

_____

_____

_____

_____

➢ Highlight a passage that speaks to you.

➢ Write a thought God gave to you.

_____

_____

_____

Prayer Prompts:

➢ Praise God as the God of your country.

➢ Confess sins your country has committed.

➢ Confess sins you committed today.

➢ Pray for your country to turn back to God.

➢ Pray for the needs of someone else.

➢ Pray for something you need today.

Day 164: Jeremiah 21:1 – 7

Bible Study:

➤ Double underline God's words.

➤ What is the prophecy?

_____

_____

_____

_____

_____

_____

➤ How would you react if you found out your country was going to be attacked?

_____

_____

_____

_____

_____

➤ Highlight a passage that speaks to you.

➤ Write a thought God gave to you.

_____

_____

_____

Prayer Prompts:

➤ Praise God for protecting your country.

➤ Confess ignoring prophecies.

➤ Confess sins you committed today.

➤ Pray for your enemies.

➤ Pray for the needs of someone else.

➤ Pray for something you need today.

Day 165: 2 Kings 23:36 – 24:14

Bible Study:

- Put an exclamation point (!) next to what Jehoikim did.

- Put an exclamation point (!) next to what Jehoiachin did.

- Why did God allow Judah to be attacked?

_____

_____

_____

_____

_____

- Highlight a passage that speaks to you.

- Write a thought God gave to you.

_____

_____

_____

Prayer Prompts:

- Praise God for keeping His word.

- Confess not understanding God's actions.

- Confess sins you committed today.

- Pray for His protection on your country.

- Pray for the needs of someone else.

- Pray for something you need today.

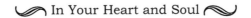

Day 166: Jeremiah 39:1 – 18

Bible Study:

➢ Put an exclamation point (!) next to what Nebuchadnezzar did.

➢ How did Nebuchadnezzar treat Jeremiah?

_____

_____

_____

➢ How has God protected you?

_____

_____

_____

_____

➢ Highlight a passage that speaks to you.

➢ Write a thought God gave to you.

_____

_____

_____

Prayer Prompts:

➢ Praise God for His protection.

➢ Confess not understanding God's actions.

➢ Confess sins you committed today.

➢ Pray for His protection on your country.

➢ Pray for the needs of someone else.

➢ Pray for something you need today.

Day 167: Isaiah 14:1 – 9

Bible Study:

➢ Underline and define words you do not know.

_____

_____

_____

➢ Put a squiggle line under how the earth praises God.

➢ Put an arrow next to the hope.

➢ Highlight a passage that speaks to you.

➢ Write a thought God gave to you.

_____

_____

_____

Prayer Prompts:

➢ Praise God for something you love in nature.

➢ Confess sorrow and fear.

➢ Confess sins you committed today.

➢ Pray for rest and hope.

➢ Pray for the needs of someone else.

➢ Pray for something you need today.

Day 168: Ezekiel 1:1 – 3, & 9:1 – 11

Bible Study:

➢ Double underline God's words.

➢ Put a squiggle line under Ezekiel's prayer.

➢ Do you pray for sinners? _____

➢ Highlight a passage that speaks to you.

➢ Write a thought God gave to you.

_____

_____

_____

Prayer Prompts:

➢ Praise God for mercy.

➢ Confess judgement of others.

➢ Confess sins you committed today.

➢ Pray for those that you think do not deserve mercy. Pray for a change in your mindset towards those people.

➢ Pray for the needs of someone else.

➢ Pray for something you need today.

Day 169: Daniel 1:1 – 21

Bible Study:

➤ Circle Daniel's actions.

➤ Put an X next to what happened to Daniel and his friends.

➤ What was Daniel's character?

_____

_____

_____

➤ Highlight a passage that speaks to you.

➤ Write a thought God gave to you.

_____

_____

_____

Prayer Prompts:

➤ Praise God for His favor.

➤ Confess lack of courage.

➤ Confess sins you committed today.

➤ Pray for favor with God and man.

➤ Pray for the needs of someone else.

➤ Pray for something you need today.

Day 170: Daniel 2:1 – 23

Bible Study:

- Box the king's actions.
- Double star the blessing from God.
- Can God do the impossible?

_____

_____

_____

- Highlight a passage that speaks to you.
- Write a thought God gave to you.

_____

_____

_____

Prayer Prompts:

- Praise God for being all-powerful.
- Confess doubting God's power.
- Confess sins you committed today.
- Pray for the impossible.
- Pray for the needs of someone else.
- Pray for something you need today.

Day 171: Daniel 2:24 – 49

Bible Study:

- ➢ Put a squiggle line under how Daniel gave praise to God.
- ➢ Double underline the prophetic dream.
- ➢ Put a squiggle line under Nebuchadnezzar's praise of God.
- ➢ Put an X next to what happened to Daniel.
- ➢ Highlight a passage that speaks to you.
- ➢ Write a thought God gave to you.

_____

_____

_____

Prayer Prompts:

- ➢ Praise God for the talents He gave you.
- ➢ Confess not using your talents for God.
- ➢ Confess sins you committed today.
- ➢ Pray for guidance for how to use your talents.
- ➢ Pray for the needs of someone else.
- ➢ Pray for something you need today.

Day 172: Daniel 3:1 – 30

Bible Study:

➢ Put an exclamation point (!) next to what Nebuchadnezzar did.

➢ Circle what Shadrach, Meshach, and Obednego did.

➢ Put an X next to what happened to them.

➢ Put a double star next to the miracle.

➢ Put a squiggle line under Nebuchadnezzar's praise.

➢ Highlight a passage that speaks to you.

➢ Write a thought God gave to you.

_____

_____

_____

Prayer Prompts:

➢ Praise God for sending His Son to die for your sins.

➢ Confess giving in to peer pressure.

➢ Confess sins you committed today.

➢ Pray for boldness to stand for God.

➢ Pray for the needs of someone else.

➢ Pray for something you need today.

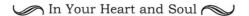

Day 173: Daniel 4:4 – 27

Bible Study:

➢ Double underline Nebuchadnezzar's prophetic dream.

➢ What was the interpretation of the dream?

_____

_____

_____

_____

_____

_____

➢ How could he have prevented the dream from coming true?

_____

_____

_____

_____

➢ Highlight a passage that speaks to you.

➢ Write a thought God gave to you.

_____

_____

_____

Prayer Prompts:

➢ Praise God for the warnings He gives us.

➢ Confess ignoring God's corrections.

➢ Confess sins you committed today.

➢ Pray for an obedient spirit.

➢ Pray for the needs of someone else.

➢ Pray for something you need today.

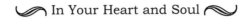

Day 174: Daniel 4:28 – 37

Bible Study:

- ➤ Put an exclamation point (!) next to Nebuchadnezzar's pride.
- ➤ Put an X next to what happened to him.
- ➤ Put a squiggle line under his praise.
- ➤ Did he learn his lesson?

_____

_____

_____

_____

_____

_____

_____

_____

_____

_____

_____

- ➤ Highlight a passage that speaks to you.
- ➤ Write a thought God gave to you.

_____

_____

_____

Prayer Prompts:

- ➤ Praise God for His corrections.
- ➤ Confess pride.
- ➤ Confess sins you committed today.
- ➤ Pray for mercy and grace in your life.
- ➤ Pray for the needs of someone else.
- ➤ Pray for something you need today.

Day 175: Daniel 5:1 – 14

Bible Study:

➤ Put an exclamation point (!) next to what Belshazzar did.

➤ Put a double star next to what God did.

➤ Put an arrow next to Daniel's good testimony.

➤ What do unsaved people know about you?

_____

_____

_____

_____

_____

_____

_____

_____

_____

_____

_____

➤ Highlight a passage that speaks to you.

➤ Write a thought God gave to you.

_____

_____

_____

Prayer Prompts:

➤ Praise God for miracles.

➤ Confess disrespect towards God.

➤ Confess sins you committed today.

➤ Pray for a good testimony.

➤ Pray for the needs of someone else.

➤ Pray for something you need today.

Day 176: Daniel 5:15 – 31

Bible Study:

➢ Underline and define words you do not know.

_____

_____

_____

➢ Put an exclamation point (!) next to Belshazzar's sin.

➢ Double underline the meaning of the writing on the wall.

➢ Put an X next to what happened to Belshazzar.

➢ Highlight a passage that speaks to you.

➢ Write a thought God gave to you.

_____

_____

_____

Prayer Prompts:

➢ Praise God for knowing the past, present, and future.

➢ Confess pride.

➢ Confess sins you committed today.

➢ Pray for guidance for your future.

➢ Pray for the needs of someone else.

➢ Pray for something you need today.

Day 177: Daniel 6:1 – 14

Bible Study:

➢ Put an arrow next to the favor shown to Daniel.

➢ Put an exclamation point (!) next to the plot against Daniel.

➢ Circle Daniel's faith.

➢ Put a squiggle line under how Daniel prayed.

➢ Put an X next to the king's regret.

➢ Have you ever been tricked into doing something wrong?

_____

_____

_____

_____

_____

➢ Highlight a passage that speaks to you.

➢ Write a thought God gave to you.

_____

_____

_____

Prayer Prompts:

➢ Praise God for all He has done for you.

➢ Confess giving in to peer pressure.

➢ Confess sins you committed today.

➢ Pray for courage to take a stand for God.

➢ Pray for the needs of someone else.

➢ Pray for something you need today.

Day 178: Daniel 6:15 – 28

Bible Study:

➢ Put an exclamation point (!) next to the plot against Daniel.

➢ Circle the faith of the king.

➢ Double star the miracle.

➢ Put an X next to what happened to Daniel.

➢ Highlight a passage that speaks to you.

➢ Write a thought God gave to you.

_____

_____

_____

Prayer Prompts:

➢ Praise God for His protection.

➢ Confess doubts.

➢ Confess sins you committed today.

➢ Pray for a faith like Daniel's.

➢ Pray for the needs of someone else.

➢ Pray for something you need today.

Day 179: Esther 1:1 – 20

Bible Study:

- ➤ Put an exclamation point (!) next to the drunkenness.
- ➤ Put an exclamation point (!) next to Vashti's refusals.
- ➤ Put an X next to what happened to the queen.
- ➤ Highlight a passage that speaks to you.
- ➤ Write a thought God gave to you.

_____

_____

_____

Prayer Prompts:

- ➤ Praise God for working behind the scenes.
- ➤ Confess disobedience.
- ➤ Confess sins you committed today.
- ➤ Pray for unsaved people in your country.
- ➤ Pray for the needs of someone else.
- ➤ Pray for something you need today.

Day 180: Esther 2:1 – 20

Bible Study:

➤ Put an arrow next to the kindness of the keeper of women.

➤ Circle Esther's obedience.

➤ Put an X next to what happened to Esther.

➤ How do you feel about Christians in political positions?

_____

_____

_____

_____

_____

_____

_____

_____

➤ Highlight a passage that speaks to you.

➤ Write a thought God gave to you.

_____

_____

_____

Prayer Prompts:

➤ Praise God for the help He gives you with your school or career.

➤ Confess selfishness.

➤ Confess sins you committed today.

➤ Pray for someone who has been kind to you.

➤ Pray for the needs of someone else.

➤ Pray for something you need today.

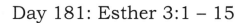

Day 181: Esther 3:1 – 15

Bible Study:

➤ Circle Mordecai's courage.

➤ Put an exclamation point (!) next to Haman's anger and plan.

➤ How do you respond to evil authority figures?

_____

_____

_____

_____

_____

_____

_____

_____

_____

➤ Highlight a passage that speaks to you.

➤ Write a thought God gave to you.

_____

_____

_____

Prayer Prompts:

➤ Praise God for good authority figures.

➤ Confess anger controlling your actions.

➤ Confess sins you committed today.

➤ Pray for those in authority over you.

➤ Pray for the needs of someone else.

➤ Pray for something you need today.

Day 182: Esther 4:1 – 17

Bible Study:

➤ How do you express sadness?

_____

_____

_____

_____

➤ What is your first reaction when something upsets you?

_____

_____

_____

_____

➤ Highlight Mordecai's response to Esther.

➤ Circle Esther's bravery.

➤ Put a squiggle line under how the people prayed.

➤ Highlight a passage that speaks to you.

➤ Write a thought God gave to you.

_____

_____

_____

Prayer Prompts:

➤ Praise God as the God of all comfort.

➤ Confess not noticing sadness in others.

➤ Confess sins you committed today.

➤ Pray for courage.

➤ Pray for the needs of someone else.

➤ Pray for something you need today.

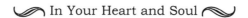

Day 183: Esther 5:1 – 14

Bible Study:

➢ What did Esther do before she confronted the king.?

_____

_____

_____

_____

➢ Put an arrow next to the favor shown to Esther.

➢ Why do you think Esther asked for the banquets?

_____

_____

_____

_____

_____

➢ Put an exclamation point (!) next to Haman's indignation.

➢ Highlight a passage that speaks to you.

➢ Write a thought God gave to you.

_____

_____

_____

Prayer Prompts:

➢ Praise God for someone that has shown you favor.

➢ Confess indignation.

➢ Confess sins you committed today.

➢ Pray for good relationships with others.

➢ Pray for the needs of someone else.

➢ Pray for something you need today.

Day 184: Esther 6:1 – 14

Bible Study:

➤ Put an arrow next to what Mordecai did.

➤ Put an exclamation point (!) next to Haman's pride.

➤ Put an exclamation point (!) next to Haman's plan.

➤ Put an X next to what happened to Mordecai.

➤ How do you show gratitude to people?

_____

_____

_____

_____

_____

➤ Highlight a passage that speaks to you.

➤ Write a thought God gave to you.

_____

_____

_____

Prayer Prompts:

➤ Praise God for people that help you.

➤ Confess pride.

➤ Confess sins you committed today.

➤ Pray for someone that has done something for you.

➤ Pray for the needs of someone else.

➤ Pray for something you need today.

Decision:

➤ Can you show your gratitude to someone that has done something for you?

_____

_____

_____

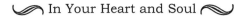

Day 185: Esther 7:1 - 10

Bible Study:

➢ Put a star next to how Esther made her request.

➢ Put an X next to what happened to Haman.

➢ How was Esther wise?

_____

_____

_____

➢ How do you ask for things?

_____

_____

_____

_____

➢ Highlight a passage that speaks to you.

➢ Write a thought God gave to you.

_____

_____

_____

Prayer Prompts:

➢ Praise God for His guidance.

➢ Confess asking with selfishness.

➢ Confess sins you committed today.

➢ Pray for wisdom.

➢ Pray for the needs of someone else.

➢ Pray for something you need today.

Decision:

➢ Can you change how you ask for things?

_____

_____

_____

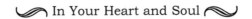

Day 186: Esther 8:1 – 17

Bible Study:

➤ Put an X next to what happened to Mordecai.

➤ Put an arrow next to the king's new decree.

➤ How were the Jews saved?

_____

_____

_____

_____

➤ How did God take care of His people?

_____

_____

_____

_____

_____

➤ Highlight a passage that speaks to you.

➤ Write a thought God gave to you.

_____

_____

_____

Prayer Prompts:

➤ Praise God for taking care of His people.

➤ Confess hopelessness.

➤ Confess sins you committed today.

➤ Pray for guidance in your actions.

➤ Pray for the needs of someone else.

➤ Pray for something you need today.

Day 187: Ezra 1:1 – 11

Bible Study:

➤ Double star the fulfilled prophecy.

➤ What prophecy was Cyrus fulfilling.?

_____

_____

_____

➤ What were the people supposed to build?

_____

_____

_____

_____

_____

➤ Highlight a passage that speaks to you.

➤ Write a thought God gave to you.

_____

_____

_____

Prayer Prompts:

➤ Praise God for fulfilled prophecies.

➤ Confess ignoring the needs of your church.

➤ Confess sins you committed today.

➤ Pray for the needs of your church.

➤ Pray for the needs of someone else.

➤ Pray for something you need today.

Decision:

➤ Can you do something to meet a need at your church?

_____

_____

_____

Day 188: Ezra 3:8 – 13 & 6:13 – 22

Bible Study:

➢ Put an arrow next to the attitude of the workers.

➢ Put an exclamation point (!) next to the attitude of the workers.

➢ Put a squiggle line under how the people praised God.

➢ How do you help your church?

_____

➢ What is your attitude towards helping your church?

_____

_____

_____

_____

➢ Highlight a passage that speaks to you.

➢ Write a thought God gave to you.

_____

_____

_____

Prayer Prompts:

➢ Praise God for your church.

➢ Confess a bad attitude.

➢ Confess sins you committed today.

➢ Pray for a way to help your church.

➢ Pray for the needs of someone else.

➢ Pray for something you need today.

Decision:

➢ Can you change your attitude at church?

_____

_____

_____

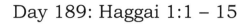

Day 189: Haggai 1:1 – 15

Bible Study:

- ➤ Double underline God's words.
- ➤ Put an exclamation point (!) next to what the people did.
- ➤ Put an X next to what the Lord did to the people.
- ➤ Circle Zerubbabel's obedience.
- ➤ Do you care more about your house or the Lord's house?

_____

_____

_____

_____

_____

_____

- ➤ Highlight a passage that speaks to you.
- ➤ Write a thought God gave to you.

_____

_____

_____

Prayer Prompts:

- ➤ Praise God for your pastor.
- ➤ Confess caring more about your house than the Lord's house.
- ➤ Confess sins you committed today.
- ➤ Pray for God's power on your church.
- ➤ Pray for the needs of someone else.
- ➤ Pray for something you need today.

Decision:

- ➤ What is a way you can care for your church?

_____

_____

_____

Day 190: Haggai 2:1 – 9

Bible Study:

- ➢ Double underline God's words.
- ➢ Double star the blessing.
- ➢ Who does the church belong to?

_____

_____

_____

_____

_____

_____

- ➢ Highlight a passage that speaks to you.
- ➢ Write a thought God gave to you.

_____

_____

_____

Prayer Prompts:

- ➢ Praise God for owning your church.
- ➢ Confess working in your own power.
- ➢ Confess sins you committed today.
- ➢ Pray for the Lord to build His church.
- ➢ Pray for the needs of someone else.
- ➢ Pray for something you need today.

Decision:

- ➢ How can you help build your church?

_____

_____

_____

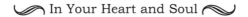

Day 191: Zechariah 8:1 – 13

Bible Study:

➢ Who is speaking? _____

➢ Double underline God's words.

➢ Who does the Lord want to change?

_____

_____

_____

_____

_____

_____

➢ Highlight a passage that speaks to you.

➢ Write a thought God gave to you.

_____

_____

_____

Prayer Prompts:

➢ Praise God for being all-powerful.

➢ Confess your weaknesses.

➢ Confess sins you committed today.

➢ Pray for strong hands.

➢ Pray for the needs of someone else.

➢ Pray for something you need today.

Day 192: Zechariah 9:1 – 17

Bible Study:

➢ Put an exclamation point (!) next to what Tyrus did.

➢ Put an X next to what happened to Tyrus.

➢ Double underline the prophecy.

➢ Put a squiggle line under how he praised God.

➢ Highlight a passage that speaks to you.

➢ Write a thought God gave to you.

_____

_____

_____

Prayer Prompts:

➢ Praise God for His goodness and His beauty.

➢ Confess greed.

➢ Confess sins you committed today.

➢ Pray that you will keep your eyes on God.

➢ Pray for the needs of someone else.

➢ Pray for something you need today.

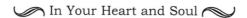

Day 193: Nehemiah 1:1 & 2:1 – 6

Bible Study:

➢ Who is speaking? _____

➢ Put a squiggle line under how he prayed.

➢ Do you notice sadness in others?

_____

_____

_____

_____

➢ Highlight a passage that speaks to you.

➢ Write a thought God gave to you.

_____

_____

_____

Prayer Prompts:

➢ Praise God for hearing your cries.

➢ Confess ignoring sadness in others.

➢ Confess sins you committed today.

➢ Pray for something that makes you sad.

➢ Pray for the needs of someone else.

➢ Pray for something you need today.

Decision:

➢ Who is someone you have noticed is sad? Can you help them?

_____

_____

_____

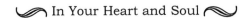

Day 194: Nehemiah 2:11 – 18

Bible Study:

- ➤ Who is speaking? _____
- ➤ To whom is he speaking? _____
- ➤ What did he want them to do?

  _____

  _____

  _____

  _____

- ➤ What is something God has given you a passion for?

  _____

  _____

  _____

- ➤ Highlight a passage that speaks to you.
- ➤ Write a thought God gave to you.

  _____

  _____

  _____

Prayer Prompts:

- ➤ Praise God for the passion He has given you.
- ➤ Confess not working on those passions.
- ➤ Confess sins you committed today.
- ➤ Pray for more passion.
- ➤ Pray for the needs of someone else.
- ➤ Pray for something you need today.

Decision:

- ➤ What can you do to work on the passion God gave you?

  _____

  _____

  _____

Day 195: Nehemiah 4:1 – 17

Bible Study:

➤ Put an exclamation point (!) next to what Sanballat did.

➤ Put a squiggle line under what Nehemiah did when the others conspired against Jerusalem.

➤ Put a squiggle line under how Nehemiah described God.

➤ Circle their courage.

➤ How do you respond to criticism?

_____

_____

_____

_____

➤ Highlight a passage that speaks to you.

➤ Write a thought God gave to you.

_____

_____

Prayer Prompts:

➤ Praise God as the Great and Terrible and the One who fights for you.

➤ Confess indignation towards someone else's success.

➤ Confess sins you committed today.

➤ Pray for courage against naysayers.

➤ Pray for the needs of someone else.

➤ Pray for something you need today.

Decision:

➤ Have you ever stopped doing something because others discouraged you? Decide to start doing it again.

_____

_____

_____

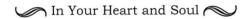

Day 196: Malachi 1:1 – 14

Bible Study:

➢ Who is speaking? _____

➢ Double underline God's words.

➢ Put a squiggle line under the definitions of God.

➢ Highlight a passage that speaks to you.

➢ Write a thought God gave to you.

_____

_____

_____

Prayer Prompts:

➢ Praise God using the definitions of God in this passage.

➢ Confess not honoring God.

➢ Confess sins you committed today.

➢ Pray for His name to be magnified on Earth.

➢ Pray for the needs of someone else.

➢ Pray for something you need today.

Day 197: Malachi 3:1 – 6

Bible Study:

➤ Double underline the prophecy.

➤ Put a squiggle line under the description of God.

➤ Do you know what New Testament person this passage is about?

_____

➤ Highlight a passage that speaks to you.

➤ Write a thought God gave to you.

_____

_____

_____

Prayer Prompts:

➤ Praise God for never changing.

➤ Confess lying.

➤ Confess sins you committed today.

➤ Pray for God to use you.

➤ Pray for the needs of someone else.

➤ Pray for something you need today.

Day 198: Luke 1:5 – 25

Bible Study:

➢ Circle the description of Zacharias and Elizabeth.

➢ Put a squiggle line under how they prayed.

➢ Double star the answered prayer.

➢ Double underline the prophecy.

➢ Put an exclamation point (!) next to Zacharias' doubt.

➢ Put an X next to what happened to him.

➢ Highlight a passage that speaks to you.

➢ Write a thought God gave to you.

_____

_____

_____

Prayer Prompts:

➢ Praise God for answered prayer. (Be specific)

➢ Confess doubt.

➢ Confess sins you committed today.

➢ Pray for something you think is impossible.

➢ Pray for the needs of someone else.

➢ Pray for something you need today.

Day 199: Luke 1:26 – 47

Bible Study:

➢ Double underline the prophecy.

➢ Circle the description of Mary.

➢ Double star the miracles.

➢ Highlight a passage that speaks to you.

➢ Write a thought God gave to you.

_____

_____

_____

➢ Memorize verse 37.

Prayer Prompts:

➢ Praise God for doing the impossible.

➢ Confess unbelief.

➢ Confess sins you committed today.

➢ Pray for faith to see the impossible.

➢ Pray for the needs of someone else.

➢ Pray for something you need today.

Decision:

➢ Decide to pray for the impossible.

_____

_____

_____

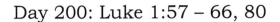

Day 200: Luke 1:57 – 66, 80

Bible Study:

- ➤ Put an arrow next to the mercy shown to Elizabeth.
- ➤ Box how Zacharias' answered the people.
- ➤ Put a squiggle line under how the people rejoiced.
- ➤ Highlight a passage that speaks to you.
- ➤ Write a thought God gave to you.

_____

_____

_____

Prayer Prompts:

- ➤ Praise God for a miracle you have seen.
- ➤ Confess working against God's will.
- ➤ Confess sins you committed today.
- ➤ Pray that you will work towards the goals God has for you.
- ➤ Pray for the needs of someone else.
- ➤ Pray for something you need today.

Day 201: Matthew 1:18 – 25

Bible Study:

➢ Underline and define words you do not know.

_____

_____

_____

➢ Circle the description of Joseph.

➢ Put an arrow next to the kindness Joseph planned for Mary.

➢ Double underline the prophecy.

➢ Circle Joseph's obedience.

➢ Highlight a passage that speaks to you.

➢ Write a thought God gave to you.

_____

_____

_____

Prayer Prompts:

➢ Praise God for kind people.

➢ Confess judging others.

➢ Confess sins you committed today.

➢ Pray for someone you may have misjudged.

➢ Pray for the needs of someone else.

➢ Pray for something you need today.

Decision:

➢ Decide to give that person another chance.

_____

_____

_____

Day 202: Luke 2:1 – 20

Bible Study:

➤ Box what caused them to go to Bethlehem.

➤ Why was it important that Jesus was from David's lineage?

_____

_____

_____

➤ Double star the miracles.

➤ Put a squiggle line under the angel's praise.

➤ Put a squiggle line under the shepherd's praise.

➤ Highlight a passage that speaks to you.

➤ Write a thought God gave to you.

_____

_____

_____

Prayer Prompts:

➤ Praise God by saying, "Glory to God in the highest."

➤ Confess disobeying authority.

➤ Confess sins you committed today.

➤ Pray for salvation for someone you know.

➤ Pray for the needs of someone else.

➤ Pray for something you need today.

Day 203: Luke 2:21 – 40

Bible Study:

➤ Put a squiggle line under how they praised.

➤ Double underline the prophecy.

➤ Put a squiggle line under how Anna prayed.

➤ Do you get excited when someone gets saved?

_____

_____

_____

➤ Highlight a passage that speaks to you.

➤ Write a thought God gave to you.

_____

_____

_____

➤ Memorize verse 30.

Prayer Prompts:

➤ Praise God for something He promised you.

➤ Confess not witnessing more.

➤ Confess sins you committed today.

➤ Pray for people in your town to get saved.

➤ Pray for the needs of someone else.

➤ Pray for something you need today.

Day 204: Matthew 2:1 – 12

Bible Study:

➢ Circle the description of the men from the east.

➢ Double underline what was written by the prophets.

➢ Put an exclamation point (!) next to Herod's lie.

➢ Put a squiggle line under the wise men's joy and how they worshipped.

➢ Double underline the warning from God.

➢ What gifts can you give to Jesus?

_____

_____

_____

➢ Highlight a passage that speaks to you.

➢ Write a thought God gave to you.

_____

_____

_____

Prayer Prompts:

➢ Praise God for sending Jesus.

➢ Confess holding your gifts back from God.

➢ Confess sins you committed today.

➢ Pray for Jesus to guide your steps.

➢ Pray for the needs of someone else.

➢ Pray for something you need today.

Decision:

➢ Decide to give a gift to Jesus.

_____

_____

_____

Day 205: Matthew 2:13 – 23

Bible Study:

- ➢ Double underline God's protection.
- ➢ Circle Joseph's obedience.
- ➢ Double underline what the prophet said.
- ➢ Put an exclamation point (!) next to what Herod did.
- ➢ Highlight a passage that speaks to you.
- ➢ Write a thought God gave to you.

_____

_____

_____

Prayer Prompts:

- ➢ Praise God for His protection.
- ➢ Confess not following God's guidance.
- ➢ Confess sins you committed today.
- ➢ Pray for someone that needs to hear about Jesus.
- ➢ Pray for the needs of someone else.
- ➢ Pray for something you need today.

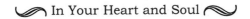

Day 206: Luke 2:41 – 52

Bible Study:

➢ Underline and define words you do not know.

_____

_____

_____

➢ How long would you go without Jesus?

_____

_____

_____

_____

➢ Where was Jesus and what was He doing?

_____

_____

_____

_____

➢ Highlight a passage that speaks to you.

➢ Write a thought God gave to you.

_____

_____

_____

➢ Memorize verse 52.

Prayer Prompts:

➢ Praise God for how Jesus works in your life.

➢ Confess forgetting Jesus.

➢ Confess sins you committed today.

➢ Pray that you will increase in wisdom, and stature, and in favor with God and man.

➢ Pray for the needs of someone else.

➢ Pray for something you need today.

Day 207: Mark 1:1 – 8

Bible Study:

➢ Underline and define words you do not know.

_____

_____

_____

➢ Double underline what was said by the prophets.

➢ Put a squiggle line under how John the Baptist described Jesus.

➢ Highlight a passage that speaks to you.

➢ Write a thought God gave to you.

_____

_____

_____

Prayer Prompts:

➢ Praise Jesus for His mighty power.

➢ Confess pride.

➢ Confess sins you committed today.

➢ Pray for someone that needs to be baptized.

➢ Pray for the needs of someone else.

➢ Pray for something you need today.

Decision:

➢ What decision have you made?

_____

_____

_____

Day 208: Luke 3:1 – 14

Bible Study:

➤ Double underline the prophecy.

➤ Put an arrow next to the kind things John the Baptist told people to do.

➤ Write verses 11, 13, & 14 in your own words:

_____

_____

_____

_____

_____

_____

_____

_____

➤ Highlight a passage that speaks to you.

➤ Write a thought God gave to you.

_____

_____

_____

Prayer Prompts:

➤ Praise God for prophecies.

➤ Confess how you treat people.

➤ Confess sins you committed today.

➤ Pray for someone you have been upset with.

➤ Pray for the needs of someone else.

➤ Pray for something you need today.

Decision:

➤ Decide to be nicer to people.

_____

_____

_____

Day 209: Matthew 3:13 – 17

Bible Study:

➢ Underline and define words you do not know.

_____

_____

_____

➢ What was John's reaction?

_____

_____

_____

➢ Double underline God's words.

➢ Highlight a passage that speaks to you.

➢ Write a thought God gave to you.

_____

_____

_____

➢ Memorize verse 17.

Prayer Prompts:

➢ Praise God for sending His Beloved Son.

➢ Confess disagreeing with God.

➢ Confess sins you committed today.

➢ Pray for Jesus to be magnified.

➢ Pray for the needs of someone else.

➢ Pray for something you need today.

Day 210: Matthew 4:1 – 11

Bible Study:

➤ Put a squiggle line under how Jesus prepared to be tempted.

➤ Put an exclamation point (!) next to how Satan tempted Jesus.

➤ Double underline the scripture Jesus used in response.

➤ Double star how the angel's ministered to Jesus.

➤ Highlight a passage that speaks to you.

➤ Write a thought God gave to you.

_____

_____

_____

Prayer Prompts:

➤ Praise Jesus for experiencing and defeating temptation.

➤ Confess giving in to temptation.

➤ Confess sins you committed today.

➤ Pray for help when you are tempted.

➤ Pray for the needs of someone else.

➤ Pray for something you need today.

Decision:

➤ How will you face temptation from now on?

_____

_____

_____

Day 211: Mark 1:14 -22, Matthew 9:9, & Luke 6:12 - 16

Bible Study:

➤ Double underline Jesus' words.

➤ Circle the obedience of the disciples.

➤ Put a star next to how Jesus taught.

➤ Put a squiggle line under how Jesus prayed.

➤ What did Jesus do before choosing His disciples?

_____

_____

_____

➤ Highlight a passage that speaks to you.

➤ Write a thought God gave to you.

_____

_____

_____

Prayer Prompts:

➤ Praise God for your friends.

➤ Confess allowing bad influences in your life.

➤ Confess sins you committed today.

➤ Pray for your friends.

➤ Pray for the needs of someone else.

➤ Pray for something you need today.

Decision:

➤ Decide how you will let new friends into your life.

_____

_____

_____

Day 212: Matthew 5:1 – 12

Bible Study:

➢ Double underline Jesus' words.

➢ Circle the attitudes.

➢ Put an X next to what happens to those with each attitude.

➢ Highlight a passage that speaks to you.

➢ Write a thought God gave to you.

_____

_____

_____

Prayer Prompts:

➢ Praise God for the blessings He gives you.

➢ Confess bad attitudes.

➢ Confess sins you committed today.

➢ Pray for blessings.

➢ Pray for the needs of someone else.

➢ Pray for something you need today.

Decision:

➢ Which attitudes would you like to develop?

_____

_____

_____

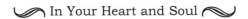

Day 213: Matthew 6:1 – 4

Bible Study:

➤ Underline and define words you do not know.

_____

_____

➤ Double underline Jesus' words.

➤ What good works do you do?

_____

_____

➤ How do you do your good works?

_____

_____

_____

➤ Highlight a passage that speaks to you.

➤ Write a thought God gave to you.

_____

_____

_____

Prayer Prompts:

➤ Praise God for blessing our good works.

➤ Confess doing good works for man's praise.

➤ Confess sins you committed today.

➤ Pray for a good spirit.

➤ Pray for the needs of someone else.

➤ Pray for something you need today.

Decision:

➤ How will you do good works?

_____

_____

_____

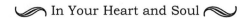

Day 214: Luke 11:1 – 13

Bible Study:

➤ Double underline Jesus' words.

➤ Write the example prayer in your own words:

_____

_____

_____

_____

_____

_____

➤ What attitude should you have while praying?

_____

_____

➤ Highlight a passage that speaks to you.

➤ Write a thought God gave to you.

_____

_____

➤ Memorize verses 9 – 10.

Prayer Prompts:

➤ Praise God for the example prayer.

➤ Confess unforgiveness.

➤ Confess sins you committed today.

➤ Pray for something you have never asked for before.

➤ Pray for the needs of someone else.

➤ Pray for something you need today.

Decision:

➤ Decide to be more persistent in your prayers.

_____

_____

_____

Day 215: John 2:1 – 11

Bible Study:

➤ Underline and define words you do not know.

_____

_____

_____

➤ Double underline Jesus' words.

➤ Circle the servant's obedience.

➤ Double star the miracle.

➤ Why did Jesus do miracles?

_____

_____

_____

➤ Highlight a passage that speaks to you.

➤ Write a thought God gave to you.

_____

_____

_____

Prayer Prompts:

➤ Praise God for His glory being magnified on Earth.

➤ Confess disobedience.

➤ Confess sins you committed today.

➤ Pray for God to use you in His miracles.

➤ Pray for the needs of someone else.

➤ Pray for something you need today.

Decision:

➤ How can you help God with a miracle?

_____

_____

_____

Day 216: Luke 4:14 – 29

Bible Study:

➢ Double underline God's words.

➢ Put an exclamation point (!) next to the people's doubt.

➢ Put an exclamation point (!) next to their wrath.

➢ Does your family seem to have less faith in you than others?

_____

_____

_____

_____

➢ Highlight a passage that speaks to you.

➢ Write a thought God gave to you.

_____

_____

_____

Prayer Prompts:

➢ Praise God for His power on your life.

➢ Confess doubting Gd's power on others.

➢ Confess sins you committed today.

➢ Pray for God to build you up.

➢ Pray for the needs of someone else.

➢ Pray for something you need today.

Decision:

➢ Who do you need to believe in more?

_____

_____

_____

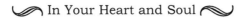

Day 217: Mark 6:7 – 13

Bible Study:

➢ Underline and define words you do not know.

_____

_____

➢ Star Jesus' instructions.

➢ What did they preach?

_____

➢ What else did they do?

_____

_____

➢ How were they supposed to act when someone would not receive them?

_____

_____

➢ Highlight a passage that speaks to you.

➢ Write a thought God gave to you.

_____

_____

Prayer Prompts:

➢ Praise God for preaching.

➢ Confess discouragement.

➢ Confess sins you committed today.

➢ Pray for more opportunities to witness to others.

➢ Pray for the needs of someone else.

➢ Pray for something you need today.

Decision:

➢ How will you react to people that try to discourage you?

_____

_____

_____

Day 218: John 3:1 – 21

Bible Study:

➤   Double underline Jesus' words.

➤   What did Nicodemus ask?

_____

_____

_____

_____

➤   What does the term, "born again," mean?

_____

_____

_____

➤   Highlight a passage that speaks to you.

➤   Write a thought God gave to you.

_____

_____

_____

➤   Memorize verse 16.

Prayer Prompts:

➤   Praise God for salvation and the ability to go to Heaven.

➤   Confess not telling others how to go to Heaven.

➤   Confess sins you committed today.

➤   Pray for someone that needs to be saved.

➤   Pray for the needs of someone else.

➤   Pray for something you need today.

Decision:

➤   Who can you tell about salvation?

_____

_____

_____

Day 219: John 4:3 – 42

Bible Study:

- Double underline Jesus' words.
- Put an arrow next to what Jesus needed to do.
- What example did Jesus give of salvation.?

_____

_____

_____

- Circle what the woman did after Jesus spoke to her.
- What did Jesus compare witnessing to?

_____

_____

_____

- Highlight a passage that speaks to you.
- Write a thought God gave to you.

_____

_____

_____

Prayer Prompts:

- Praise Jesus as the Savior of the world.
- Confess your attitude towards witnessing.
- Confess sins you committed today.
- Pray for someone you can witness to.
- Pray for the needs of someone else.
- Pray for something you need today.

Decision:

- Who do you know that needs to be saved?

_____

_____

_____

Day 220: John 4:43 – 54

Bible Study:

➢ Double underline Jesus' words.

➢ Circle the noble man's belief.

➢ Double star the miracle.

➢ Highlight a passage that speaks to you.

➢ Write a thought God gave to you.

_____

_____

_____

Prayer Prompts:

➢ Praise God for a miracle you have seen.

➢ Confess unbelief.

➢ Confess sins you committed today.

➢ Pray for a miracle to happen in your life.

➢ Pray for the needs of someone else.

➢ Pray for something you need today.

Decision:

➢ What decision have you made?

_____

_____

_____

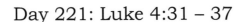

Day 221: Luke 4:31 – 37

Bible Study:

- ➤ Circle the description of Jesus' word.
- ➤ Put an exclamation point (!) next to what the man with the unclean spirit said.
- ➤ Double underline Jesus' words.
- ➤ Double star the miracle.
- ➤ Highlight a passage that speaks to you.
- ➤ Write a thought God gave to you.

_____

_____

_____

Prayer Prompts:

- ➤ Praise God for the fame of Jesus.
- ➤ Confess a sin God has laid on your heart.
- ➤ Confess sins you committed today.
- ➤ Pray for your city to be saved.
- ➤ Pray for the needs of someone else.
- ➤ Pray for something you need today.

Decision:

- ➤ What decision have you made?

_____

_____

_____

Day 222: Mark 1:29 – 36

Bible Study:

➤ Underline and define words you do not know.

_____

_____

_____

➤ Double star the miracle.

➤ Put a squiggle line under how He prayed.

➤ Double underline Jesus' words.

➤ Highlight a passage that speaks to you.

➤ Write a thought God gave to you.

_____

_____

_____

Prayer Prompts:

➤ Praise God for His healing power.

➤ Confess doubt.

➤ Confess sins you committed today.

➤ Pray for someone that is sick.

➤ Pray for the needs of someone else.

➤ Pray for something you need today.

Decision:

➤ What decision have you made?

_____

_____

_____

Day 223: Luke 5:1 – 11

Bible Study:

➢ Double underline Jesus' words.

➢ Put an exclamation point (!) next to Simon Peter's excuses.

➢ Double star the miracle.

➢ Put a squiggle line under how Simon Peter worshiped.

➢ What did Jesus mean by, "catch men?"

_____

_____

_____

_____

_____

_____

➢ Highlight a passage that speaks to you.

➢ Write a thought God gave to you.

_____

_____

_____

Prayer Prompts:

➢ Praise God for being worthy of worship.

➢ Confess unworthiness.

➢ Confess sins you committed today.

➢ Pray for an opportunity to witness.

➢ Pray for the needs of someone else.

➢ Pray for something you need today.

Decision:

➢ What decision have you made?

_____

_____

_____

Day 224: Mark 1:40 – 45

Bible Study:

➢ Circle the Leper's faith.

➢ Put an arrow next to how Jesus felt.

➢ Double underline Jesus' words.

➢ Double star the miracle.

➢ Highlight a passage that speaks to you.

➢ Write a thought God gave to you.

_____

_____

_____

Prayer Prompts:

➢ Praise God for His compassion.

➢ Confess unbelief.

➢ Confess sins you committed today.

➢ Pray for someone that is sick.

➢ Pray for the needs of someone else.

➢ Pray for something you need today.

Decision:

➢ What decision have you made?

_____

_____

_____

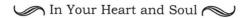

Day 225: Luke 7:1 – 10

Bible Study:

- ➢ Circle the centurion's persistence.
- ➢ Circle the centurion's faith.
- ➢ Double underline Jesus' words.
- ➢ How does your faith compare to the centurion's?

_____

_____

_____

_____

_____

_____

_____

- ➢ Highlight a passage that speaks to you.
- ➢ Write a thought God gave to you.

_____

_____

_____

Prayer Prompts:

- ➢ Praise God for an answered prayer.
- ➢ Confess a lack of faith.
- ➢ Confess sins you committed today.
- ➢ Pray for more faith.
- ➢ Pray for the needs of someone else.
- ➢ Pray for something you need today.

Decision:

- ➢ What decision have you made?

_____

_____

_____

Day 226: Luke 5:17 – 26

Bible Study:

➢ Circle the act of the friends.

➢ Double underline Jesus' words.

➢ Double star the miracle.

➢ How was the lame man affected by the faith of his friends?

_____

_____

_____

_____

_____

_____

_____

➢ Highlight a passage that speaks to you.

➢ Write a thought God gave to you.

_____

_____

_____

Prayer Prompts:

➢ Praise God for good friends.

➢ Confess skepticism.

➢ Confess sins you committed today.

➢ Pray for your friends.

➢ Pray for the needs of someone else.

➢ Pray for something you need today.

Decision:

➢ What decision have you made?

_____

_____

_____

Day 227: Luke 7:11 – 17

Bible Study:

- ➤ Circle how Jesus felt about the widow's son.
- ➤ Double underline Jesus' words.
- ➤ Double star the miracle.
- ➤ Put a squiggle line under how the people worshiped.
- ➤ Highlight a passage that speaks to you.
- ➤ Write a thought God gave to you.

_____

_____

_____

Prayer Prompts:

- ➤ Praise God for His greatness.
- ➤ Confess a sin God has laid on your heart.
- ➤ Confess sins you committed today.
- ➤ Pray for compassion.
- ➤ Pray for the needs of someone else.
- ➤ Pray for something you need today.

Decision:

- ➤ What decision have you made?

_____

_____

_____

Day 228: Mark 4:1 – 20

Bible Study:

➢ Underline and define words you do not know.

_____

_____

_____

➢ Double underline Jesus' words.

➢ What is the seed?

_____

_____

➢ Write this parable in your own words.

_____

_____

_____

➢ Highlight a passage that speaks to you.

➢ Write a thought God gave to you.

_____

_____

Prayer Prompts:

➢ Praise God as your teacher.

➢ Confess having a stony heart.

➢ Confess sins you committed today.

➢ Pray for a soft heart.

➢ Pray for the needs of someone else.

➢ Pray for something you need today.

Decision:

➢ What decision have you made?

_____

_____

_____

Day 229: Mark 4:21 – 29

Bible Study:

➤ Double underline Jesus' words.

➤ What is the candle a picture of?

_____

_____

➤ What are we not supposed to do to the candle?

_____

_____

➤ How does this apply to your life?

_____

_____

_____

➤ Highlight a passage that speaks to you.

➤ Write a thought God gave to you.

_____

_____

_____

Prayer Prompts:

➤ Praise God for the Bible.

➤ Confess hiding your testimony.

➤ Confess sins you committed today.

➤ Pray for boldness to witness to others.

➤ Pray for the needs of someone else.

➤ Pray for something you need today.

Decision:

➤ What decision have you made?

_____

_____

_____

Day 230: Mark 4:35 – 41

Bible Study:

➤ Double underline Jesus' words.

➤ Put an exclamation point (!) next to the disciple's fear.

➤ Double star the miracle.

➤ Who is someone that needs to hear this story?

_____

_____

_____

_____

➤ Highlight a passage that speaks to you.

➤ Write a thought God gave to you.

_____

_____

_____

Prayer Prompts:

➤ Praise God for being all-powerful.

➤ Confess fear.

➤ Confess sins you committed today.

➤ Pray for a miracle you want to see.

➤ Pray for the needs of someone else.

➤ Pray for something you need today.

Decision:

➤ What decision have you made?

_____

_____

_____

Day 231: Luke 8:26 – 39

Bible Study:

- ➢ Put an exclamation point (!) next to what was wrong with the man.
- ➢ How did the man react to Jesus?

_____

_____

_____

- ➢ Double underline Jesus' words.
- ➢ Double star the miracle.
- ➢ Put an X next to what happened to the Legion.
- ➢ Put a squiggle line under how the man praised Jesus.
- ➢ Highlight a passage that speaks to you.
- ➢ Write a thought God gave to you.

_____

_____

_____

Prayer Prompts:

- ➢ Praise God for deliverance from evil.
- ➢ Confess being around the wrong influences.
- ➢ Confess sins you committed today.
- ➢ Pray for someone that is going down the wrong path.
- ➢ Pray for the needs of someone else.
- ➢ Pray for something you need today.

Decision:

- ➢ What decision have you made?

_____

_____

_____

Day 232: Mark 5:21 – 42

Bible Study:

- ➢ Put a squiggle line under how Jairus worshiped.
- ➢ Circle the act of the woman.
- ➢ Double underline Jesus' words.
- ➢ Double star the miracles.
- ➢ Highlight a passage that speaks to you.
- ➢ Write a thought God gave to you.

_____

_____

_____

Prayer Prompts:

- ➢ Praise God for an answered prayer.
- ➢ Confess impatience with God's timing.
- ➢ Confess sins you committed today.
- ➢ Pray for someone that needs to be healed.
- ➢ Pray for the needs of someone else.
- ➢ Pray for something you need today.

Decision:

- ➢ What decision have you made?

_____

_____

_____

Day 233: Matthew 9:27 – 31

Bible Study:

➤ Circle the blind man's faith.

➤ Double underline Jesus' words.

➤ Double star the miracle.

➤ Put a squiggle line under how they praised.

➤ Highlight a passage that speaks to you.

➤ Write a thought God gave to you.

_____

_____

_____

Prayer Prompts:

➤ Praise God for the good things He has done for you.

➤ Confess keeping blessings to yourself.

➤ Confess sins you committed today.

➤ Pray for someone that needs a blessing.

➤ Pray for the needs of someone else.

➤ Pray for something you need today.

Decision:

➤ What decision have you made?

_____

_____

_____

Day 234: John 5:1 – 16

Bible Study:

➢ Underline and define words you do not know.

_____

_____

➢ Double underline Jesus' words.

➢ Double star the miracle.

➢ Put an exclamation point (!) next to what the Jews said about the miracle.

➢ Why did the Jews decide to persecute Jesus?

_____

_____

➢ Have you ever been persecuted for doing something good?

_____

_____

➢ Highlight a passage that speaks to you.

➢ Write a thought God gave to you.

_____

_____

Prayer Prompts:

➢ Praise God for something miraculous in your life.

➢ Confess judging others.

➢ Confess sins you committed today.

➢ Pray for deliverance from those that would persecute you.

➢ Pray for the needs of someone else.

➢ Pray for something you need today.

Decision:

➢ What decision have you made?

_____

_____

_____

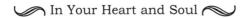

Day 235: Luke 8:4 – 18

Bible Study:

➢ Underline and define words you do not know.

_____

_____

➢ Double underline Jesus' words.

➢ What is the seed?

_____

_____

➢ What are each of the grounds?

_____

_____

_____

➢ Highlight a passage that speaks to you.

➢ Write a thought God gave to you.

_____

_____

_____

Prayer Prompts:

➢ Praise Jesus for being a teacher.

➢ Confess not having a soft heart.

➢ Confess sins you committed today.

➢ Pray for someone to witness to.

➢ Pray for the needs of someone else.

➢ Pray for something you need today.

Decision:

➢ What decision have you made?

_____

_____

_____

Day 236: Matthew 13:24 – 30, 36 – 43

Bible Study:

➤ Put an exclamation point (!) next to the enemy that sowed the tares.

➤ Who is the sower? _____

➤ What is the field? _____

➤ Who is the good seed? _____

➤ Who is the enemy? _____

➤ Who are the tares? _____

➤ Who are the reapers? _____

➤ Why are evil people allowed to live with good people?

_____

_____

➤ When will this change? _____

➤ Highlight a passage that speaks to you.

➤ Write a thought God gave to you.

_____

_____

Prayer Prompts:

➤ Praise God for His timing.

➤ Confess frustrations.

➤ Confess sins you committed today.

➤ Pray for people to hear the Word of God.

➤ Pray for the needs of someone else.

➤ Pray for something you need today.

Decision:

➤ What decision have you made?

_____

_____

_____

Day 237: John 6:1 – 15

Bible Study:

- ➤ Double underline Jesus' words.
- ➤ What did Jesus do before the miracle?

_____

_____

_____

- ➤ Double star the miracle.
- ➤ Why did Jesus leave?

_____

_____

- ➤ What should you do before attempting something big for God?

_____

_____

- ➤ Highlight a passage that speaks to you.
- ➤ Write a thought God gave to you.

_____

_____

Prayer Prompts:

- ➤ Praise God for His power.
- ➤ Confess doubts.
- ➤ Confess sins you committed today.
- ➤ Pray for something big you can do for God.
- ➤ Pray for the needs of someone else.
- ➤ Pray for something you need today.

Decision:

- ➤ What decision have you made?

_____

_____

_____

Day 238: Matthew 14:22 – 33

Bible Study:

➤ Put a squiggle line under how Jesus prayed.

➤ Double star the miracle.

➤ Put an exclamation point (!) next to the disciples' fear.

➤ Double underline Jesus' words.

➤ Why did Peter start to sink?

_____

_____

➤ Put a squiggle line under how the disciples worshiped.

➤ Has your life ever been affected when you took your eyes off Jesus?

_____

_____

➤ Highlight a passage that speaks to you.

➤ Write a thought God gave to you.

_____

_____

_____

Prayer Prompts:

➤ Praise Jesus as the Son of God.

➤ Confess taking your eyes off Jesus.

➤ Confess sins you committed today.

➤ Pray that you will keep your eyes on Jesus.

➤ Pray for the needs of someone else.

➤ Pray for something you need today.

Decision:

➤ What decision have you made?

_____

_____

_____

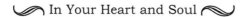

Day 239: Matthew 15:1 – 20

Bible Study:

➢ Put an exclamation point (!) next to the disciples' fear.

➢ Double underline Jesus' words.

➢ How did Jesus respond to them? _____

➢ How did they feel about Jesus' answer?

_____

➢ What comes from the heart? _____

➢ What was Jesus' thought about the unwashed hands?

_____

_____

➢ What does "hypocrite" mean?

_____

_____

➢ Highlight a passage that speaks to you.

➢ Write a thought God gave to you.

_____

_____

Prayer Prompts:

➢ Praise God for understanding your heart.

➢ Confess hypocrisy.

➢ Confess sins you committed today.

➢ Pray for Jesus to fight your battles.

➢ Pray for the needs of someone else.

➢ Pray for something you need today.

Decision:

➢ What decision have you made?

_____

_____

_____

Day 240: Matthew 15:21 – 31

Bible Study:

➤ Put a squiggle line under how the woman prayed.

➤ Circle the woman's faith.

➤ Double underline Jesus' words.

➤ Double star the miracles.

➤ What was different about this woman?

_____

_____

_____

_____

_____

➤ Highlight a passage that speaks to you.

➤ Write a thought God gave to you.

_____

_____

_____

Prayer Prompts:

➤ Praise God for treating everyone equally.

➤ Confess lack of faith.

➤ Confess sins you committed today.

➤ Pray for someone that needs to be healed.

➤ Pray for the needs of someone else.

➤ Pray for something you need today.

Decision:

➤ What decision have you made?

_____

_____

_____

Day 241: Mark 7:31 – 37

Bible Study:

➢ Underline and define words you do not know.

_____

_____

➢ Double underline Jesus' words.

➢ Double star the miracle.

➢ Put a squiggle line under how they praised.

➢ Can you keep quiet about the things God does for you?

_____

_____

➢ Who do you need to tell about God's goodness?

_____

➢ Highlight a passage that speaks to you.

➢ Write a thought God gave to you.

_____

_____

_____

Prayer Prompts:

➢ Praise God for His miracles.

➢ Confess not telling others about Jesus' goodness.

➢ Confess sins you committed today.

➢ Pray for someone that needs to hear about miracles.

➢ Pray for the needs of someone else.

➢ Pray for something you need today.

Decision:

➢ What decision have you made?

_____

_____

_____

Day 242: Mark 8:1 – 9

Bible Study:

- ➢ Double underline Jesus' words.
- ➢ Circle how Jesus felt about the people.
- ➢ Double star the miracle.
- ➢ Put a squiggle line under when Jesus prayed.
- ➢ What miracle have you seen?

_____

_____

_____

_____

_____

- ➢ Highlight a passage that speaks to you.
- ➢ Write a thought God gave to you.

_____

_____

_____

Prayer Prompts:

- ➢ Praise God for His compassion.
- ➢ Confess not acknowledging the miracles of God.
- ➢ Confess sins you committed today.
- ➢ Pray for compassion towards others.
- ➢ Pray for the needs of someone else.
- ➢ Pray for something you need today.

Decision:

- ➢ What decision have you made?

_____

_____

_____

Day 243: Mark 8:22 – 26

Bible Study:

➢ Underline and define words you do not know.

_____

_____

_____

➢ Double star the miracle.

➢ Does God always give you a clear vision of what is going on?

_____

_____

_____

_____

➢ Highlight a passage that speaks to you.

➢ Write a thought God gave to you.

_____

_____

_____

Prayer Prompts:

➢ Praise God for being all-knowing.

➢ Confess something God has laid on your heart.

➢ Confess sins you committed today.

➢ Pray for clear vision in your life.

➢ Pray for the needs of someone else.

➢ Pray for something you need today.

Decision:

➢ What decision have you made?

_____

_____

_____

Day 244: John 9:1 – 20

Bible Study:

- ➢ What was the disciples' question?

  _____

- ➢ Double underline Jesus' words.
- ➢ Why was the man blind?

  _____

  _____

- ➢ Double star the miracle.
- ➢ Put a squiggle line under how the man praised.
- ➢ Put an exclamation point (!) next to how the Pharisees criticized.
- ➢ Why does God allow bad things to happen?

  _____

  _____

- ➢ Highlight a passage that speaks to you.
- ➢ Write a thought God gave to you.

  _____

  _____

Prayer Prompts:

- ➢ Praise God for something He has done in your life.
- ➢ Confess criticizing other Christians.
- ➢ Confess sins you committed today.
- ➢ Pray for Jesus to be magnified in your life.
- ➢ Pray for the needs of someone else.
- ➢ Pray for something you need today.

Decision:

- ➢ What decision have you made?

  _____

  _____

  _____

Day 245: John 10:1 – 21

Bible Study:

➤ Double underline Jesus' words.

➤ Who is the door? _____

➤ Who are the thieves and robbers? _____

➤ Who are the sheep? _____

➤ Put an exclamation point (!) next to what the wolf does.

➤ What did Jesus say He was going to do?

_____

_____

➤ Put an exclamation point (!) next to how the people reacted.

➤ Highlight a passage that speaks to you.

➤ Write a thought God gave to you.

_____

_____

➤ Memorize verse 10.

Prayer Prompts:

➤ Praise Jesus for being the door to Heaven.

➤ Confess listening to a thief.

➤ Confess sins you committed today.

➤ Pray for someone that needs to be saved.

➤ Pray for the needs of someone else.

➤ Pray for something you need today.

Decision:

➤ What decision have you made?

_____

_____

_____

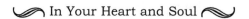

Day 246: Matthew 16:1 – 12

Bible Study:

➢ Underline and define words you do not know.

_____

_____

_____

➢ Put an exclamation point (!) next to what the Pharisees and Sadducees did wrong.

➢ Double underline Jesus' words.

➢ How many baskets were left over?

_____

➢ What does the leaven represent?

_____

_____

➢ Highlight a passage that speaks to you.

➢ Write a thought God gave to you.

_____

_____

_____

Prayer Prompts:

➢ Praise God for the Bible.

➢ Confess hypocrisy.

➢ Confess sins you committed today.

➢ Pray that you will stay away from false teachers.

➢ Pray for the needs of someone else.

➢ Pray for something you need today.

Decision:

➢ What decision have you made?

_____

_____

_____

Day 247: Matthew 17:1 – 13

Bible Study:

➢ Underline and define words you do not know.

_____

_____

➢ How did Jesus change?

_____

_____

_____

➢ Double star the miracle.

➢ Double underline God's words.

➢ Put a squiggle line under how the disciples worshiped.

➢ Double underline Jesus' words.

➢ Highlight a passage that speaks to you.

➢ Write a thought God gave to you.

_____

_____

_____

Prayer Prompts:

➢ Praise Jesus as the Son of God.

➢ Confess not fearing God.

➢ Confess sins you committed today.

➢ Pray for your town to hear about Jesus.

➢ Pray for the needs of someone else.

➢ Pray for something you need today.

Decision:

➢ What decision have you made?

_____

_____

_____

Day 248: Matthew 17:14 – 21

Bible Study:

➤ Underline and define words you do not know.

_____

_____

_____

➤ Double underline Jesus' words.

➤ Double star the miracle.

➤ Why couldn't the disciples heal the boy?

_____

_____

_____

➤ Put a squiggle line under how you get faith.

➤ Highlight a passage that speaks to you.

➤ Write a thought God gave to you.

_____

_____

_____

Prayer Prompts:

➤ Praise God for healing.

➤ Confess lack of faith.

➤ Confess sins you committed today.

➤ Pray for more faith.

➤ Pray for the needs of someone else.

➤ Pray for something you need today.

Decision:

➤ What decision have you made?

_____

_____

_____

Day 249: Luke 10:25 – 37

Bible Study:

- ➤ Put an exclamation point (!) next to what the lawyer did.

- ➤ Double underline Jesus' words.

- ➤ How did Jesus respond to the lawyer?

  _____

- ➤ What was the lawyer's attitude?

  _____

  _____

- ➤ Put an exclamation point (!) next to what the thieves did.

- ➤ Put an exclamation point (!) next to what the priest did.

- ➤ Put an exclamation point (!) next to what the Levite did.

- ➤ Circle what the Samaritan did.

- ➤ Who is your neighbor? _____

- ➤ Highlight a passage that speaks to you.

- ➤ Write a thought God gave to you.

  _____

  _____

Prayer Prompts:

- ➤ Praise God for someone that was merciful to you.

- ➤ Confess not treating everyone like your neighbor.

- ➤ Confess sins you committed today.

- ➤ Pray for your neighbor.

- ➤ Pray for the needs of someone else.

- ➤ Pray for something you need today.

Decision:

- ➤ What decision have you made?

  _____

  _____

  _____

Day 250: Luke 10:38 – 42

Bible Study:

➢ Underline and define words you do not know.

_____

_____

➢ Put a squiggle line under how Mary worshiped.

➢ Put a squiggle line under how Martha worshiped.

➢ Put an exclamation point (!) next to Martha's attitude.

➢ Double underline Jesus' words.

➢ How did Jesus respond to Martha?

_____

_____

_____

➢ Highlight a passage that speaks to you.

➢ Write a thought God gave to you.

_____

_____

_____

Prayer Prompts:

➢ Praise God for how He rebukes you.

➢ Confess a bad attitude about serving.

➢ Confess sins you committed today.

➢ Pray that you will choose the good part of worship.

➢ Pray for the needs of someone else.

➢ Pray for something you need today.

Decision:

➢ What decision have you made?

_____

_____

_____

Day 251: Matthew 17:24 – 27

Bible Study:

- Underline and define words you do not know.

_____

_____

_____

- Double underline Jesus' words.
- Double star the miracle.
- Highlight a passage that speaks to you.
- Write a thought God gave to you.

_____

_____

_____

Prayer Prompts:

- Praise God for providing for your needs.
- Confess something God has laid on your heart.
- Confess sins you committed today.
- Pray for money you need.
- Pray for the needs of someone else.
- Pray for something you need today.

Decision:

- What decision have you made?

_____

_____

_____

Day 252: Luke 12:22 – 34

Bible Study:

➢ Underline and define words you do not know.

_____

_____

➢ Double underline Jesus' words.

➢ Put an exclamation point (!) next to the worries.

➢ What does worrying do for you?

_____

_____

➢ How are your needs met?

_____

_____

➢ Highlight a passage that speaks to you.

➢ Write a thought God gave to you.

_____

_____

_____

Prayer Prompts:

➢ Praise God as your caring Father.

➢ Confess worries.

➢ Confess sins you committed today.

➢ Pray for God to take away your worries.

➢ Pray for the needs of someone else.

➢ Pray for something you need today.

Decision:

➢ What decision have you made?

_____

_____

_____

Day 253: Luke 13:22 – 30

Bible Study:

➤ Double underline Jesus' words.

➤ Will everyone who claims they are going to Heaven really go?

_____

_____

_____

_____

➤ How do you go to Heaven?

_____

_____

_____

_____

➤ Highlight a passage that speaks to you.

➤ Write a thought God gave to you.

_____

_____

_____

Prayer Prompts:

➤ Praise Jesus for salvation.

➤ Confess not telling others how to go to Heaven.

➤ Confess sins you committed today.

➤ Pray for someone that needs to be told how to go to Heaven.

➤ Pray for the needs of someone else.

➤ Pray for something you need today.

Decision:

➤ What decision have you made?

_____

_____

_____

Day 254: Luke 15:1 – 10

Bible Study:

- ➢ Circle what the publicans and sinners did.
- ➢ Put an exclamation point (!) next to the attitude of the Pharisees and Scribes.
- ➢ Double underline Jesus' words.
- ➢ Rewrite these parables in your own words:

_____

_____

_____

_____

_____

_____

_____

- ➢ Highlight a passage that speaks to you.
- ➢ Write a thought God gave to you.

_____

_____

_____

Prayer Prompts:

- ➢ Praise Jesus for searching for you.
- ➢ Confess something God has laid on your heart.
- ➢ Confess sins you committed today.
- ➢ Pray for a sinner that needs to be found.
- ➢ Pray for the needs of someone else.
- ➢ Pray for something you need today.

Decision:

- ➢ What decision have you made?

_____

_____

_____

Day 255: Luke 15:11 – 32

Bible Study:

- ➤ Double underline Jesus' words.
- ➤ Put an exclamation point (!) next to the actions of the Prodigal Son.
- ➤ Circle the Prodigal Son's wise decision.
- ➤ Circle how the father reacted to his son.
- ➤ Put an exclamation point (!) next to the reaction of the older brother.
- ➤ How do you act when someone who has messed up returns to church?

_____

_____

_____

_____

_____

- ➤ Highlight a passage that speaks to you.
- ➤ Write a thought God gave to you.

_____

_____

Prayer Prompts:

- ➤ Praise God for His open arms.
- ➤ Confess an attitude towards people that have left the church.
- ➤ Confess sins you committed today.
- ➤ Pray for someone that is like the Prodigal Son.
- ➤ Pray for the needs of someone else.
- ➤ Pray for something you need today.

Decision:

- ➤ What decision have you made?

_____

_____

_____

Day 256: Luke 16:1 – 10

Bible Study:

➤ Underline and define words you do not know.

_____

_____

➤ Double underline Jesus' words.

➤ Put stars next to the steward's wise actions.

➤ How does this apply to your life?

_____

_____

_____

_____

➤ Highlight a passage that speaks to you.

➤ Write a thought God gave to you.

_____

_____

_____

Prayer Prompts:

➤ Praise God for the blessings He has given to you.

➤ Confess using God's gifts unjustly.

➤ Confess sins you committed today.

➤ Pray that you will use God's gifts wisely.

➤ Pray for the needs of someone else.

➤ Pray for something you need today.

Decision:

➤ What decision have you made?

_____

_____

_____

Day 257: Luke 16:19 – 31

Bible Study:

➢ Double underline Jesus' words.

➢ Put an X next too what happened to each man.

➢ What did the rich man want for his family?

_____

_____

➢ What was Abraham's response?

_____

_____

➢ What family members do you have that need to be saved?

_____

_____

➢ Highlight a passage that speaks to you.

➢ Write a thought God gave to you.

_____

_____

_____

Prayer Prompts:

➢ Praise God for the goodness of Heaven.

➢ Confess not telling your family about salvation.

➢ Confess sins you committed today.

➢ Pray for a family member that needs to be saved.

➢ Pray for the needs of someone else.

➢ Pray for something you need today.

Decision:

➢ What decision have you made?

_____

_____

_____

Day 258: Matthew 18:21 – 35

Bible Study:

➢ What was Peter's question?

_____

➢ Double underline Jesus' words.

➢ What was Jesus' answer?

_____

➢ Circle the compassion of the lord.

➢ Put an exclamation point (!) next to how the servant treated his fellow servants.

➢ Put an X next to what happened to the servant.

➢ Do you forgive others as easily as God forgave you?

_____

_____

_____

➢ Highlight a passage that speaks to you.

➢ Write a thought God gave to you.

_____

_____

Prayer Prompts:

➢ Praise God for forgiveness.

➢ Confess not forgiving others.

➢ Confess sins you committed today.

➢ Pray for a forgiving spirit.

➢ Pray for the needs of someone else.

➢ Pray for something you need today.

Decision:

➢ What decision have you made?

_____

_____

_____

Day 259: Luke 17:11 – 19

Bible Study:

- ➢ Double underline Jesus' words.
- ➢ Double star the miracle.
- ➢ Put a squiggle line under how the one thanked God.
- ➢ Do you forget to be thankful?

_____

_____

_____

_____

_____

_____

_____

- ➢ Highlight a passage that speaks to you.
- ➢ Write a thought God gave to you.

_____

_____

_____

Prayer Prompts:

- ➢ Praise God for healing.
- ➢ Confess forgetting to be thankful.
- ➢ Confess sins you committed today.
- ➢ Pray for a thankful spirit.
- ➢ Pray for the needs of someone else.
- ➢ Pray for something you need today.

Decision:

- ➢ What decision have you made?

_____

_____

_____

Day 260: Luke 18:18 – 30

Bible Study:

➢ Double underline Jesus' words.

➢ Put an exclamation point (!) next to the rich young man's attitude.

➢ Highlight a passage that speaks to you.

➢ Write a thought God gave to you.

_____

_____

_____

➢ Memorize verse 27.

Prayer Prompts:

➢ Praise Jesus as the Savior of all.

➢ Confess loving material things.

➢ Confess sins you committed today.

➢ Pray that you will follow Jesus with all your heart.

➢ Pray for the needs of someone else.

➢ Pray for something you need today.

Decision:

➢ What decision have you made?

_____

_____

_____

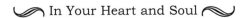

Day 261: Luke 19:1 – 10

Bible Study:

➤ Underline and define words you do not know.

_____

_____

➤ Double underline Jesus' words.

➤ Put an exclamation point (!) next to the crowd's reaction.

➤ Put a squiggle line under how Zacchaeus spoke to Jesus.

➤ Do you judge people for spending time with sinners?

_____

_____

_____

_____

➤ Highlight a passage that speaks to you.

➤ Write a thought God gave to you.

_____

_____

_____

Prayer Prompts:

➤ Praise Jesus as the Seeker of the lost.

➤ Confess judging others.

➤ Confess sins you committed today.

➤ Pray for someone that needs to be saved.

➤ Pray for the needs of someone else.

➤ Pray for something you need today.

Decision:

➤ What decision have you made?

_____

_____

_____

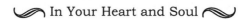

Day 262: John 11:1 – 44

Bible Study:

➢ Double underline Jesus' words.

➢ Why didn't Jesus go to Lazarus right away?

_____

_____

_____

➢ Double star the miracle.

➢ Is God ever too late?

_____

_____

_____

_____

➢ Highlight a passage that speaks to you.

➢ Write a thought God gave to you.

_____

_____

➢ Memorize verse 35.

Prayer Prompts:

➢ Praise Jesus for having power over death.

➢ Confess frustration over God's timing.

➢ Confess sins you committed today.

➢ Pray that you will trust God's timing.

➢ Pray for the needs of someone else.

➢ Pray for something you need today.

Decision:

➢ What decision have you made?

_____

_____

_____

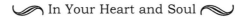

Day 263: Matthew 20:1 – 16

Bible Study:

➢ Double underline Jesus' words.

➢ Put an exclamation point (!) next to the murmurers.

➢ Why were they upset?

_____

_____

➢ What was the man's response?

_____

_____

➢ How does this apply to your life?

_____

_____

➢ Highlight a passage that speaks to you.

➢ Write a thought God gave to you.

_____

_____

_____

Prayer Prompts:

➢ Praise Jesus for treating everyone equally.

➢ Confess discontentment.

➢ Confess sins you committed today.

➢ Pray for contentment with your circumstances.

➢ Pray for the needs of someone else.

➢ Pray for something you need today.

Decision:

➢ What decision have you made?

_____

_____

_____

Day 264: Mark 10:46 – 51

Bible Study:

- ➢ Put a squiggle line under how Bartimaeus prayed.
- ➢ Double underline Jesus' words.
- ➢ Circle Bartimaeus' faith.
- ➢ Double star the miracle.
- ➢ Highlight a passage that speaks to you.
- ➢ Write a thought God gave to you.

_____

_____

_____

Prayer Prompts:

- ➢ Praise God for His mercy.
- ➢ Confess something God has laid on your heart.
- ➢ Confess sins you committed today.
- ➢ Pray for more faith.
- ➢ Pray for the needs of someone else.
- ➢ Pray for something you need today.

Decision:

- ➢ What decision have you made?

_____

_____

_____

Day 265: Mark 11:1 – 11

Bible Study:

➤ Double underline Jesus' words.

➤ Put a squiggle line under how the people worshiped.

➤ Double star the miracle.

➤ Highlight a passage that speaks to you.

➤ Write a thought God gave to you.

_____

_____

_____

Prayer Prompts:

➤ Praise God by saying, "Hosanna; Blessed is He."

➤ Confess something God has laid on your heart.

➤ Confess sins you committed today.

➤ Pray for Jesus to be magnified in your city.

➤ Pray for the needs of someone else.

➤ Pray for something you need today.

Decision:

➤ What decision have you made?

_____

_____

_____

Day 266: Mark 11:15 – 19

Bible Study:

➤ Put an exclamation point (!) next to what the moneychangers did.

➤ Put an X next to what happened to them.

➤ Double underline Jesus' words.

➤ Put an exclamation point (!) next to what the scribes and priests planned to do.

➤ What is your church like?

_____

_____

_____

_____

_____

_____

➤ Highlight a passage that speaks to you.

➤ Write a thought God gave to you.

_____

_____

_____

Prayer Prompts:

➤ Praise God as a Righteous God.

➤ Confess bitterness.

➤ Confess sins you committed today.

➤ Pray for the spirit of your church.

➤ Pray for the needs of someone else.

➤ Pray for something you need today.

Decision:

➤ What decision have you made?

_____

_____

_____

Day 267: Matthew 21:18 – 22

Bible Study:

➢ Double underline Jesus' words.

➢ Double star the miracle.

➢ What do you need to do to see a miracle?

_____

_____

_____

_____

_____

_____

_____

_____

➢ Highlight a passage that speaks to you.

➢ Write a thought God gave to you.

_____

_____

_____

Prayer Prompts:

➢ Praise God for being all-powerful.

➢ Confess lack of faith.

➢ Confess sins you committed today.

➢ Pray for more faith.

➢ Pray for the needs of someone else.

➢ Pray for something you need today.

Decision:

➢ What decision have you made?

_____

_____

_____

Day 268: Matthew 21:33 – 46

Bible Study:

- ➤ Double underline Jesus' words.
- ➤ Put an exclamation point (!) next to what the husbandmen did.
- ➤ To whom is Jesus speaking?

_____

_____

- ➤ Put an X next to what will happen to those that reject Jesus.
- ➤ How does this apply to your life?

_____

_____

_____

_____

- ➤ Highlight a passage that speaks to you.
- ➤ Write a thought God gave to you.

_____

_____

_____

Prayer Prompts:

- ➤ Praise Jesus for being sent to save us.
- ➤ Confess not bearing fruit for Jesus.
- ➤ Confess sins you committed today.
- ➤ Pray for the Jewish people.
- ➤ Pray for the needs of someone else.
- ➤ Pray for something you need today.

Decision:

- ➤ What decision have you made?

_____

_____

_____

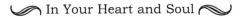

Day 269: Luke 21:1 – 4

Bible Study:

➢ Underline and define words you do not know.

_____

_____

➢ Put a squiggle line under how the widow gave.

➢ Double underline Jesus' words.

➢ Do you give out of your abundance?

_____

_____

_____

_____

_____

➢ Highlight a passage that speaks to you.

➢ Write a thought God gave to you.

_____

_____

_____

Prayer Prompts:

➢ Praise God for recognizing our gifts.

➢ Confess only giving out of your abundance.

➢ Confess sins you committed today.

➢ Pray for faith to give more.

➢ Pray for the needs of someone else.

➢ Pray for something you need today.

Decision:

➢ What decision have you made?

_____

_____

_____

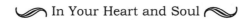

Day 270: Matthew 22:1 – 14

Bible Study:

- ➢ Double underline Jesus' words.
- ➢ Who is the king? _____
- ➢ Put an exclamation point (!) next to the people that were invited but would not come.
- ➢ Put an X next to what happened to them.
- ➢ Put an exclamation point (!) next to how the one guest was dressed.
- ➢ Put an X next to what happened to him.
- ➢ Why were these guests unworthy?

  _____

- ➢ Are you worthy of Heaven?

  _____

  _____

- ➢ Highlight a passage that speaks to you.
- ➢ Write a thought God gave to you.

  _____

  _____

Prayer Prompts:

- ➢ Praise God as your King.
- ➢ Confess your unworthiness.
- ➢ Confess sins you committed today.
- ➢ Pray for worthiness.
- ➢ Pray for the needs of someone else.
- ➢ Pray for something you need today.

Decision:

- ➢ What decision have you made?

  _____

  _____

  _____

Day 271: Mark 12:28 – 34

Bible Study:

➤ Underline and define words you do not know.

_____

_____

➤ Double underline Jesus' words.

➤ What is the first commandment? _____

➤ What is the second commandment? _____

➤ Do you follow both commandments?

_____

_____

_____

➤ Highlight a passage that speaks to you.

➤ Write a thought God gave to you.

_____

_____

_____

Prayer Prompts:

➤ Praise God by telling Him you love Him.

➤ Confess not keeping both commandments.

➤ Confess sins you committed today.

➤ Pray that you will love the Lord with all your heart, soul, mind, and strength; and that you will love your neighbor as yourself.

➤ Pray for the needs of someone else.

➤ Pray for something you need today.

Decision:

➤ What decision have you made?

_____

_____

_____

Day 272: Matthew 25:14 – 30

Bible Study:

➢ Double underline Jesus' words.

➢ Circle what the first two servants did with their talents.

➢ Put an exclamation point (!) next to what the third servant did with his talent.

➢ Put an X next to what happened to each of them.

➢ What do you do with the talents God gives you?

_____

_____

_____

_____

_____

_____

➢ Highlight a passage that speaks to you.

➢ Write a thought God gave to you.

_____

_____

_____

Prayer Prompts:

➢ Praise God for giving you talents.

➢ Confess misusing your talents.

➢ Confess sins you committed today.

➢ Pray for wisdom to use your talents righteously.

➢ Pray for the needs of someone else.

➢ Pray for something you need today.

Decision:

➢ What decision have you made?

_____

_____

_____

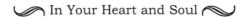

Day 273: Matthew 26:1 – 5

Bible Study:

➤ Double underline Jesus' words.

➤ Put an exclamation point (!) next to what they planned to do to Jesus.

➤ Did Jesus know what was going to happen?

_____

_____

_____

_____

_____

_____

_____

➤ Highlight a passage that speaks to you.

➤ Write a thought God gave to you.

_____

_____

_____

Prayer Prompts:

➤ Praise God for being all-knowing.

➤ Confess something God has laid on your heart.

➤ Confess sins you committed today.

➤ Pray for someone that you can tell about salvation.

➤ Pray for the needs of someone else.

➤ Pray for something you need today.

Decision:

➤ What decision have you made?

_____

_____

_____

Day 274: John 12:1 – 11

Bible Study:

- ➢ Put a squiggle line under how Mary worshiped Jesus.
- ➢ Put an exclamation point (!) next to Judas' attitude.
- ➢ Double underline Jesus' words.
- ➢ Put an exclamation point (!) next to what the chief priests planned to do.
- ➢ Highlight a passage that speaks to you.
- ➢ Write a thought God gave to you.

_____

_____

_____

Prayer Prompts:

- ➢ Praise Jesus for being Holy.
- ➢ Confess greed.
- ➢ Confess sins you committed today.
- ➢ Pray for something God has laid on your heart.
- ➢ Pray for the needs of someone else.
- ➢ Pray for something you need today.

Decision:

- ➢ What decision have you made?

_____

_____

_____

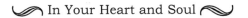

Day 275: Matthew 26:14 – 25

Bible Study:

- ➤ Put an exclamation point (!) next to what Judas and the priests did.
- ➤ Double underline Jesus' words.
- ➤ Circle the obedience of the disciples.
- ➤ Why did Judas ask Jesus if it was him?

_____

_____

_____

_____

_____

_____

- ➤ Highlight a passage that speaks to you.
- ➤ Write a thought God gave to you.

_____

_____

_____

Prayer Prompts:

- ➤ Praise God for knowing your heart.
- ➤ Confess something God has laid on your heart.
- ➤ Confess sins you committed today.
- ➤ Pray for someone that needs to open their heart to Jesus.
- ➤ Pray for the needs of someone else.
- ➤ Pray for something you need today.

Decision:

- ➤ What decision have you made?

_____

_____

_____

Day 276: John 13:1 – 17

Bible Study:

➤ Circle how Jesus felt about His followers.

➤ Double underline Jesus' words.

➤ Did Peter understand what Jesus was trying to do?

_____

_____

➤ How does this apply to your life?

_____

_____

_____

_____

➤ Highlight a passage that speaks to you.

➤ Write a thought God gave to you.

_____

_____

_____

Prayer Prompts:

➤ Praise Jesus for washing away our sins.

➤ Confess something God has laid on your heart.

➤ Confess sins you committed today.

➤ Pray that you will understand the scriptures.

➤ Pray for the needs of someone else.

➤ Pray for something you need today.

Decision:

➤ What decision have you made?

_____

_____

_____

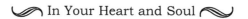

Day 277: Luke 22:24 – 30

Bible Study:

➤ Put an exclamation point (!) next to the strife.

➤ Double underline Jesus' words.

➤ Does it matter who is the greatest?

_____

_____

➤ Have you ever wondered if you were the greatest at something?

_____

_____

_____

_____

➤ Highlight a passage that speaks to you.

➤ Write a thought God gave to you.

_____

_____

_____

Prayer Prompts:

➤ Praise God for Heaven.

➤ Confess something God has laid on your heart.

➤ Confess sins you committed today.

➤ Pray for the right attitude.

➤ Pray for the needs of someone else.

➤ Pray for something you need today.

Decision:

➤ What decision have you made?

_____

_____

_____

Day 278: Matthew 26:26 – 30

Bible Study:

➢ Double underline Jesus' words.

➢ What is the bread?

_____

_____

➢ What is the cup?

_____

_____

➢ Why was Jesus' blood shed?

_____

_____

_____

➢ Highlight a passage that speaks to you.

➢ Write a thought God gave to you.

_____

_____

_____

Prayer Prompts:

➢ Praise Jesus for the reminder of salvation.

➢ Confess something God has laid on your heart.

➢ Confess sins you committed today.

➢ Pray for someone that needs to be saved.

➢ Pray for the needs of someone else.

➢ Pray for something you need today.

Decision:

➢ What decision have you made?

_____

_____

_____

Day 279: Mark 14:27 – 31

Bible Study:

➢ Double underline Jesus' words.

➢ Put an exclamation point (!) next to Peter's pride.

➢ Do you ever argue with God?

_____

_____

_____

_____

_____

_____

_____

_____

➢ Highlight a passage that speaks to you.

➢ Write a thought God gave to you.

_____

_____

Prayer Prompts:

➢ Praise God for being understanding.

➢ Confess something God has laid on your heart.

➢ Confess sins you committed today.

➢ Pray for something God has laid on your heart.

➢ Pray for the needs of someone else.

➢ Pray for something you need today.

Decision:

➢ What decision have you made?

_____

_____

_____

Day 280: John 14:1 – 31

Bible Study:

- ➢ Double underline Jesus' words.
- ➢ Put arrows next to the comfort Jesus gave.
- ➢ What should you do if you love Jesus?

_____

_____

_____

- ➢ Who is the comforter?

_____

_____

_____

- ➢ Highlight a passage that speaks to you.
- ➢ Write a thought God gave to you.

_____

_____

_____

- ➢ Memorize verse 6.

Prayer Prompts:

- ➢ Praise God for the Comforter.
- ➢ Confess something God has laid on your heart.
- ➢ Confess sins you committed today.
- ➢ Pray that you will keep the commandments.
- ➢ Pray for the needs of someone else.
- ➢ Pray for something you need today.

Decision:

- ➢ What decision have you made?

_____

_____

_____

Day 281: John 15:18 – 25

Bible Study:

➤ Double underline Jesus' words.

➤ Why does the world hate you?

_____

_____

➤ Write about a personal experience of when someone hated you. What happened, how did you feel, and was the issue resolved?

_____

_____

_____

_____

➤ Highlight a passage that speaks to you.

➤ Write a thought God gave to you.

_____

_____

_____

Prayer Prompts:

➤ Praise God as a loving God.

➤ Confess something God has laid on your heart.

➤ Confess sins you committed today.

➤ Pray that you will be a light to the world.

➤ Pray for the needs of someone else.

➤ Pray for something you need today.

Decision:

➤ What decision have you made?

_____

_____

_____

Day 282: Matthew 26:36 – 46

Bible Study:

➢ How did Jesus feel?

_____

_____

➢ Double underline Jesus' words.

➢ Put a squiggle line Jesus' prayer.

➢ Is being sorrowful wrong?

_____

_____

_____

_____

➢ Highlight a passage that speaks to you.

➢ Write a thought God gave to you.

_____

_____

_____

➢ Memorize verse 41.

Prayer Prompts:

➢ Praise God as your Father.

➢ Confess something God has laid on your heart.

➢ Confess sins you committed today.

➢ Pray for God to remove a trial you are going through.

➢ Pray for the needs of someone else.

➢ Pray for something you need today.

Decision:

➢ What decision have you made?

_____

_____

_____

Day 283: Luke 22:47 – 53

Bible Study:

➤ Double underline Jesus' words.

➤ Put an exclamation point (!) next to Judas' betrayal.

➤ Double star the miracle.

➤ How did Jesus act while being attacked?

_____

_____

➤ How do you react to being attacked?

_____

_____

_____

_____

➤ Highlight a passage that speaks to you.

➤ Write a thought God gave to you.

_____

_____

_____

Prayer Prompts:

➤ Praise God as the Son of man.

➤ Confess something God has laid on your heart.

➤ Confess sins you committed today.

➤ Pray for God to help you when you are attacked.

➤ Pray for the needs of someone else.

➤ Pray for something you need today.

Decision:

➤ What decision have you made?

_____

_____

_____

Day 284: John 18:12 – 14, Matthew 26:59 – 68, & John 18:19 – 21

Bible Study:

➤ Double underline Jesus' words.

➤ Put an exclamation point (!) next to the unfair trial tactics.

➤ How did Jesus respond?

_____

➤ Put an exclamation point (!) next to the attacks on Jesus.

➤ How do you respond to people that lie about you?

_____

_____

_____

_____

➤ Highlight a passage that speaks to you.

➤ Write a thought God gave to you.

_____

_____

_____

Prayer Prompts:

➤ Praise God for being fair.

➤ Confess something God has laid on your heart.

➤ Confess sins you committed today.

➤ Pray for the right words when facing a trial.

➤ Pray for the needs of someone else.

➤ Pray for something you need today.

Decision:

➤ What decision have you made?

_____

_____

_____

Day 285: Luke 22:54 – 62

Bible Study:

➤ Put an exclamation point (!) next to Peter's denials.

➤ Double underline the prophecy.

➤ Put an X next to how Peter reacted.

➤ Put an exclamation point (!) next to the attacks on Jesus.

➤ How do you feel after you have sinned?

_____

_____

_____

_____

_____

➤ Highlight a passage that speaks to you.

➤ Write a thought God gave to you.

_____

_____

Prayer Prompts:

➤ Praise God for forgiveness.

➤ Confess something God has laid on your heart.

➤ Confess sins you committed today.

➤ Pray for something God has laid on your heart.

➤ Pray for the needs of someone else.

➤ Pray for something you need today.

Decision:

➤ What decision have you made?

_____

_____

_____

Day 286: Mark 15:1 – 14

Bible Study:

➤ Underline and define words you do not know.

_____

_____

➤ Double underline Jesus' words.

➤ Put an exclamation point (!) next to how the chief priests influenced the people.

➤ Put an exclamation point (!) next to what the crowd wanted.

➤ Are you easily influenced by a crowd? Give a personal experience.

_____

_____

_____

_____

_____

➤ Highlight a passage that speaks to you.

➤ Write a thought God gave to you.

_____

_____

Prayer Prompts:

➤ Praise God as your King.

➤ Confess something God has laid on your heart.

➤ Confess sins you committed today.

➤ Pray for strength of character.

➤ Pray for the needs of someone else.

➤ Pray for something you need today.

Decision:

➤ What decision have you made?

_____

_____

_____

Day 287: John 19:1 – 16 & Luke 23:26 – 34

Bible Study:

➤ Put an exclamation point (!) next to how Jesus was tortured.

➤ How did Pilate try to get out of killing Jesus?

_____

➤ Double underline Jesus' words.

➤ Put an exclamation point (!) next to what the chief priests said.

➤ We often do things because we feel we have no other choice. Give a personal example of this:

_____

_____

_____

_____

➤ Highlight a passage that speaks to you.

➤ Write a thought God gave to you.

_____

_____

_____

Prayer Prompts:

➤ Praise Jesus for going through torture for you.

➤ Confess something God has laid on your heart.

➤ Confess sins you committed today.

➤ Pray that you will do the right thing despite the pressures.

➤ Pray for the needs of someone else.

➤ Pray for something you need today.

Decision:

➤ What decision have you made?

_____

_____

_____

Day 288: Luke 23:39 – 43

Bible Study:

➢ Underline and define words you do not know.

_____

_____

➢ Put a star next to the wise words of the second criminal.

➢ Double underline Jesus' words.

➢ Put an X next to what happened to that criminal.

➢ How does this apply to your life?

_____

_____

_____

_____

➢ Highlight a passage that speaks to you.

➢ Write a thought God gave to you.

_____

_____

_____

Prayer Prompts:

➢ Praise Jesus for taking you to Heaven.

➢ Confess something God has laid on your heart.

➢ Confess sins you committed today.

➢ Pray for something that God has laid on your heart.

➢ Pray for the needs of someone else.

➢ Pray for something you need today.

Decision:

➢ What decision have you made?

_____

_____

_____

Day 289: John 19:23 – 37
& Matthew 27:50 – 51

Bible Study:

➤ Put an exclamation point (!) next to what the soldiers did.

➤ Double underline the prophecy.

➤ Double underline Jesus' words.

➤ Circle how Jesus took care of His mother.

➤ Was Jesus killed or did He die through His own power?

_____

_____

_____

_____

_____

➤ Highlight a passage that speaks to you.

➤ Write a thought God gave to you.

_____

_____

_____

Prayer Prompts:

➤ Praise Jesus for His power over death.

➤ Confess something God has laid on your heart.

➤ Confess sins you committed today.

➤ Pray for your mother.

➤ Pray for the needs of someone else.

➤ Pray for something you need today.

Decision:

➤ What decision have you made?

_____

_____

_____

Day 290: Matthew 27:54 – 66

Bible Study:

➢ Put a squiggle line under the description of Jesus.

➢ Circle how Joseph took care of Jesus' body.

➢ Put an exclamation point (!) next to what the chief priests and pharisees did.

➢ How do you take care of your loved ones?

_____

_____

_____

_____

_____

_____

_____

➢ Highlight a passage that speaks to you.

➢ Write a thought God gave to you.

_____

_____

_____

Prayer Prompts:

➢ Praise Jesus as the Son of God.

➢ Confess something God has laid on your heart.

➢ Confess sins you committed today.

➢ Pray for the needs of your loved ones.

➢ Pray for the needs of someone else.

➢ Pray for something you need today.

Decision:

➢ What decision have you made?

_____

_____

_____

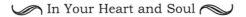

Day 291: Mark 16:1 – 10

Bible Study:

➢ Underline and define words you do not know.

_____

_____

➢ Rewrite this story as if you were one of the ones that discovered Jesus had risen from the dead:

_____

_____

_____

_____

_____

_____

➢ Highlight a passage that speaks to you.

➢ Write a thought God gave to you.

_____

_____

Prayer Prompts:

➢ Praise Jesus for dying for our sins and rising again.

➢ Confess something God has laid on your heart.

➢ Confess sins you committed today.

➢ Pray for someone that needs to hear about Jesus.

➢ Pray for the needs of someone else.

➢ Pray for something you need today.

Decision:

➢ What decision have you made?

_____

_____

_____

Day 292: John 20:1 – 18

Bible Study:

➤ Double underline Jesus' words.

➤ Double star the miracle.

➤ How did each person react to Jesus being missing?

_____

_____

➤ Put a squiggle line under how Jesus described God.

➤ How does this apply to your life?

_____

_____

_____

➤ Highlight a passage that speaks to you.

➤ Write a thought God gave to you.

_____

_____

Prayer Prompts:

➤ Praise Jesus as your Master.

➤ Confess something God has laid on your heart.

➤ Confess sins you committed today.

➤ Pray that you will understand what God is doing in your life.

➤ Pray for the needs of someone else.

➤ Pray for something you need today.

Decision:

➤ What decision have you made?

_____

_____

_____

Day 293: John 20:19 & Luke 24:36 – 47

Bible Study:

➢ Double underline Jesus' words.

➢ How did Jesus prove He was not a spirit?

_____

_____

_____

_____

➢ What do you do when you do not understand the scriptures?

_____

_____

_____

_____

➢ Highlight a passage that speaks to you.

➢ Write a thought God gave to you.

_____

_____

_____

Prayer Prompts:

➢ Praise Jesus for comforting you.

➢ Confess something God has laid on your heart.

➢ Confess sins you committed today.

➢ Pray that you will understand the scriptures.

➢ Pray for the needs of someone else.

➢ Pray for something you need today.

Decision:

➢ What decision have you made?

_____

_____

_____

Day 294: John 20:24 – 31

Bible Study:

- ➢ Put an exclamation point (!) next to Thomas' attitude.
- ➢ Double underline Jesus' words.
- ➢ Double star the miracle.
- ➢ Put a squiggle line under how Thomas praised Jesus.
- ➢ Why do we have the Bible?

_____

_____

_____

- ➢ Do you have to see something to believe it?

_____

_____

_____

- ➢ Highlight a passage that speaks to you.
- ➢ Write a thought God gave to you.

_____

_____

Prayer Prompts:

- ➢ Praise Jesus as your Lord and your God.
- ➢ Confess something God has laid on your heart.
- ➢ Confess sins you committed today.
- ➢ Pray for greater faith.
- ➢ Pray for the needs of someone else.
- ➢ Pray for something you need today.

Decision:

- ➢ What decision have you made?

_____

_____

_____

Day 295: John 21:1 – 14

Bible Study:

➢ Underline and define words you do not know.

_____

_____

➢ Double star the miracle.

➢ Double underline Jesus' words.

➢ How did Peter influence the other disciples?

_____

_____

➢ How do you influence others?

_____

_____

_____

➢ Highlight a passage that speaks to you.

➢ Write a thought God gave to you.

_____

_____

Prayer Prompts:

➢ Praise God for His miracles.

➢ Confess something God has laid on your heart.

➢ Confess sins you committed today.

➢ Pray for someone that needs encouragement.

➢ Pray for the needs of someone else.

➢ Pray for something you need today.

Decision:

➢ What decision have you made?

_____

_____

_____

Day 296: Matthew 28:16 – 20

Bible Study:

- Circle the obedience of the disciples.
- Put a squiggle line under how some worshiped Jesus.
- Put an exclamation point (!) next to the doubt.
- Double underline Jesus' words.
- Put a star next to the command Jesus gave.
- How does your church fulfill this command?

_____

_____

- How does this apply to your life?

_____

_____

_____

- Highlight a passage that speaks to you.
- Write a thought God gave to you.

_____

_____

Prayer Prompts:

- Praise God as God the Father, God the Son, and God the Holy Spirit.
- Confess something God has laid on your heart.
- Confess sins you committed today.
- Pray for an opportunity to tell others about Jesus.
- Pray for the needs of someone else.
- Pray for something you need today.

Decision:

- What decision have you made?

_____

_____

_____

In Your Heart and Soul

Day 297: Acts 1:3 – 11

Bible Study:

➤ Double underline Jesus' words.

➤ What did the disciples think was going to happen next?

_____

_____\

➤ Double star the miracle.

➤ What were the men encouraged to do?

_____

_____

➤ How often do you tell others about Jesus?

_____

_____

_____

➤ Highlight a passage that speaks to you.

➤ Write a thought God gave to you.

_____

_____

Prayer Prompts:

➤ Praise God for the Holy Ghost.

➤ Confess something God has laid on your heart.

➤ Confess sins you committed today.

➤ Pray for someone that needs to hear about Jesus.

➤ Pray for the needs of someone else.

➤ Pray for something you need today.

Decision:

➤ What decision have you made?

_____

_____

_____

Day 298: Acts 2:1 – 13

Bible Study:

➤ Underline and define words you do not know.

_____

_____

➤ Double star the miracle.

➤ Put an exclamation point (!) next to those that mocked.

➤ How does this apply to your life?

_____

_____

_____

_____

➤ Highlight a passage that speaks to you.

➤ Write a thought God gave to you.

_____

_____

_____

Prayer Prompts:

➤ Praise God for His power over languages.

➤ Confess something God has laid on your heart.

➤ Confess sins you committed today.

➤ Pray for people around the world that need to hear about Jesus.

➤ Pray for the needs of someone else.

➤ Pray for something you need today.

Decision:

➤ What decision have you made?

_____

_____

_____

Day 299: Acts 2:14 – 41

Bible Study:

➤ Underline and define words you do not know.

_____

_____

➤ Double underline the prophecy.
➤ What is your testimony?

_____

_____

_____

_____

_____

➤ Highlight a passage that speaks to you.
➤ Write a thought God gave to you.

_____

_____

➤ Memorize verse 21.

Prayer Prompts:

➤ Praise Jesus as the Christ.
➤ Confess something God has laid on your heart.
➤ Confess sins you committed today.
➤ Pray that your testimony will help someone get saved.
➤ Pray for the needs of someone else.
➤ Pray for something you need today.

Decision:

➤ What decision have you made?

_____

_____

_____

Day 300: Acts 3:1 – 11

Bible Study:

➤ Double star the miracle.

➤ Put a squiggle line under how the lame man praised.

➤ How did the man praising God affect others?

_____

_____

_____

➤ How does this apply to your life?

_____

_____

_____

_____

➤ Highlight a passage that speaks to you.

➤ Write a thought God gave to you.

_____

_____

_____

Prayer Prompts:

➤ Praise God for a miracle in your life.

➤ Confess something God has laid on your heart.

➤ Confess sins you committed today.

➤ Pray that the miracles in your life will bring others to Jesus.

➤ Pray for the needs of someone else.

➤ Pray for something you need today.

Decision:

➤ What decision have you made?

_____

_____

_____

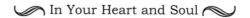

Day 301: Acts 5:1 – 11

Bible Study:

➢ Put an exclamation point (!) next to Ananias and Saphira's lie.

➢ Put an X next to what happened to them.

➢ What was Peter's question to them?

_____

_____

_____

➢ How does this apply to your life?

_____

_____

_____

_____

➢ Highlight a passage that speaks to you.

➢ Write a thought God gave to you.

_____

_____

_____

Prayer Prompts:

➢ Praise God for He is just.

➢ Confess something God has laid on your heart.

➢ Confess sins you committed today.

➢ Pray that you will be truthful in all your ways.

➢ Pray for the needs of someone else.

➢ Pray for something you need today.

Decision:

➢ What decision have you made?

_____

_____

_____

Day 302: Acts 6:8 – 15 & 7:54 – 60

Bible Study:

➢ Underline and define words you do not know.

_____

_____

➢ Circle the description of Stephen.

➢ Put an exclamation point (!) next to what the men did.

➢ How did Stephen respond to those attacking him?

_____

_____

➢ How does this apply to your life?

_____

_____

➢ Highlight a passage that speaks to you.

➢ Write a thought God gave to you.

_____

_____

_____

Prayer Prompts:

➢ Praise Jesus for His place on the right hand of God.

➢ Confess something God has laid on your heart.

➢ Confess sins you committed today.

➢ Pray for your enemies.

➢ Pray for the needs of someone else.

➢ Pray for something you need today.

Decision:

➢ What decision have you made?

_____

_____

_____

Day 303: Acts 8:1 – 14

Bible Study:

➢ Put an exclamation point (!) next to Saul's sin.

➢ Put an arrow next to what the devout men did for Stephen.

➢ Double star the miracles.

➢ Circle what Philip did.

➢ Put an X next to how the people reacted.

➢ Put an exclamation point (!) next to what Simon did.

➢ How does this apply to your life?

_____

_____

_____

_____

➢ Highlight a passage that speaks to you.

➢ Write a thought God gave to you.

_____

_____

_____

Prayer Prompts:

➢ Praise God for faithful men preaching the Bible.

➢ Confess something God has laid on your heart.

➢ Confess sins you committed today.

➢ Pray for someone that needs to get saved.

➢ Pray for the needs of someone else.

➢ Pray for something you need today.

Decision:

➢ What decision have you made?

_____

_____

_____

Day 304: Acts 8:26 – 40

Bible Study:

- ➢ Circle Philip's obedience.
- ➢ Double underline the Holy Spirit's words.
- ➢ How did Philip approach the eunuch?

_____

_____

_____

- ➢ Double star the miracle.
- ➢ How does this apply to your life?

_____

_____

_____

- ➢ Highlight a passage that speaks to you.
- ➢ Write a thought God gave to you.

_____

_____

_____

Prayer Prompts:

- ➢ Praise God for salvation.
- ➢ Confess something God has laid on your heart.
- ➢ Confess sins you committed today.
- ➢ Pray for someone you can witness to.
- ➢ Pray for the needs of someone else.
- ➢ Pray for something you need today.

Decision:

- ➢ What decision have you made?

_____

_____

_____

Day 305: Acts 9:1 – 22

Bible Study:

- ➢ Put an exclamation point (!) next to Saul's sins.
- ➢ Double star the miracles.
- ➢ Double underline Jesus' words.
- ➢ Circle Saul's repentance.
- ➢ Put an X next to what happened to Saul.
- ➢ How does this apply to your life?

_____

_____

_____

_____

- ➢ Highlight a passage that speaks to you.
- ➢ Write a thought God gave to you.

_____

_____

_____

Prayer Prompts:

- ➢ Praise God for changing your life.
- ➢ Confess something God has laid on your heart.
- ➢ Confess sins you committed today.
- ➢ Pray for someone that needs to be saved.
- ➢ Pray for the needs of someone else.
- ➢ Pray for something you need today.

Decision:

- ➢ What decision have you made?

_____

_____

_____

Day 306: Acts 10:1 – 36

Bible Study:

- ➢ Double underline Jesus' words.
- ➢ Put a squiggle line under how each man spoke to God.
- ➢ What did the vision mean?

_____

_____

_____

- ➢ How does this apply to your life?

_____

_____

_____

_____

- ➢ Highlight a passage that speaks to you.
- ➢ Write a thought God gave to you.

_____

_____

_____

Prayer Prompts:

- ➢ Praise God for being no respecter of persons.
- ➢ Confess something God has laid on your heart.
- ➢ Confess sins you committed today.
- ➢ Pray for the Word of God to reach the whole world.
- ➢ Pray for the needs of someone else.
- ➢ Pray for something you need today.

Decision:

- ➢ What decision have you made?

_____

_____

_____

Day 307: Acts 11:1 – 18

Bible Study:

➤ Underline and define words you do not know.

_____

_____

➤ Put an exclamation point (!) next to the doubts.

➤ How did Peter defend himself?

_____

_____

➤ Put a squiggle line under how they glorified God.

➤ How does this apply to your life?

_____

_____

_____

➤ Highlight a passage that speaks to you.

➤ Write a thought God gave to you.

_____

_____

Prayer Prompts:

➤ Praise God for allowing the Gospel to be for everyone.

➤ Confess something God has laid on your heart.

➤ Confess sins you committed today.

➤ Pray for a group of people that need to be saved.

➤ Pray for the needs of someone else.

➤ Pray for something you need today.

Decision:

➤ What decision have you made?

_____

_____

_____

Day 308: Acts 12:1 – 19

Bible Study:

➢ Put an exclamation point (!) next to Herod's actions.

➢ Put an exclamation point (!) next to the attitude of the Jews.

➢ Put a squiggle line under how Peter prayed.

➢ Double star the miracle.

➢ Put a squiggle line under how the people prayed.

➢ How does this apply to your life?

_____

_____

_____

_____

➢ Highlight a passage that speaks to you.

➢ Write a thought God gave to you.

_____

_____

_____

Prayer Prompts:

➢ Praise God for a miracle you have seen.

➢ Confess something God has laid on your heart.

➢ Confess sins you committed today.

➢ Pray for a friend that is being persecuted.

➢ Pray for the needs of someone else.

➢ Pray for something you need today.

Decision:

➢ What decision have you made?

_____

_____

_____

Day 309: Acts 13:42 – 52

Bible Study:

- Put an exclamation point (!) next to the envy of the Jews.
- What was Paul and Barnabas' response?

_____

_____

- Double underline the Lord's command.
- Put a squiggle line under how the Gentiles praised God.
- Put an exclamation point (!) next to the response of the Jews.
- Circle how Paul and Barnabas responded to being thrown out of the city.
- How does this apply to your life?

_____

_____

- Highlight a passage that speaks to you.
- Write a thought God gave to you.

_____

_____

_____

Prayer Prompts:

- Praise God for giving the Gospel to the Gentiles.
- Confess something God has laid on your heart.
- Confess sins you committed today.
- Pray for wisdom when you are attacked.
- Pray for the needs of someone else.
- Pray for something you need today.

Decision:

- What decision have you made?

_____

_____

_____

Day 310: James 1:1 – 27

Bible Study:

➢ Who is speaking? _____

➢ To whom is he speaking? _____

➢ Put stars next to the instructions.

➢ How does this apply to your life?

_____

_____

_____

_____

➢ Highlight a passage that speaks to you.

➢ Write a thought God gave to you.

_____

_____

_____

➢ Memorize verse 19.

Prayer Prompts:

➢ Praise God for the gifts God gives you.

➢ Confess something God has laid on your heart.

➢ Confess sins you committed today.

➢ Pray for wisdom.

➢ Pray for the needs of someone else.

➢ Pray for something you need today.

Decision:

➢ What decision have you made?

_____

_____

_____

Day 311: James 2:14 – 26

Bible Study:

- Underline and define words you do not know.

_____

_____

- What is the difference between faith and works?

_____

_____

- What is more important: faith or works?

_____

_____

- How does this apply to your life?

_____

_____

- Highlight a passage that speaks to you.
- Write a thought God gave to you.

_____

_____

Prayer Prompts:

- Praise God for honoring your faith.
- Confess something God has laid on your heart.
- Confess sins you committed today.
- Pray for a way to serve in your church.
- Pray for the needs of someone else.
- Pray for something you need today.

Decision:

- What decision have you made?

_____

_____

_____

Day 312: James 5:13 – 20

Bible Study:

➢ Put a squiggle line under the ways you are supposed to pray.

➢ Why is prayer important?

_____

_____

_____

_____

➢ How does this apply to your life?

_____

_____

_____

_____

➢ Highlight a passage that speaks to you.

➢ Write a thought God gave to you.

_____

_____

_____

Prayer Prompts:

➢ Praise God for answered prayer.

➢ Confess something God has laid on your heart.

➢ Confess sins you committed today.

➢ Pray for something God has laid on your heart.

➢ Pray for the needs of someone else.

➢ Pray for something you need today.

Decision:

➢ What decision have you made?

_____

_____

_____

Day 313: Acts 14:1 – 7 & 15:36 – 16:5

Bible Study:

- ➤ Put an exclamation point (!) next to what the unbelieving Jews did.

- ➤ Circle what the apostles did.

- ➤ What was Paul and Barnabas' fight about?

  _____

  _____

- ➤ How did they resolve their fight?

  _____

- ➤ Who was right? _____

- ➤ How does this apply to your life?

  _____

  _____

- ➤ Highlight a passage that speaks to you.

- ➤ Write a thought God gave to you.

  _____

  _____

  _____

Prayer Prompts:

- ➤ Praise God for your friends.

- ➤ Confess something God has laid on your heart.

- ➤ Confess sins you committed today.

- ➤ Pray for your relationships with your friends.

- ➤ Pray for the needs of someone else.

- ➤ Pray for something you need today.

Decision:

- ➤ What decision have you made?

  _____

  _____

  _____

Day 314: Acts 16:16 – 40

Bible Study:

➢ Put an exclamation point (!) next to what was wrong with the damsel.

➢ Double star the miracles.

➢ Put an exclamation point (!) next to what her masters did.

➢ Put an exclamation point (!) next to what the magistrates decided.

➢ Put an X next to what happened to Paul and Silas.

➢ Put an arrow next to the kindness they showed the jailer.

➢ How does this apply to your life?

_____

_____

_____

_____

➢ Highlight a passage that speaks to you.

➢ Write a thought God gave to you.

_____

_____

_____

Prayer Prompts:

➢ Praise God for power over your enemies.

➢ Confess something God has laid on your heart.

➢ Confess sins you committed today.

➢ Pray for people in law enforcement.

➢ Pray for the needs of someone else.

➢ Pray for something you need today.

Decision:

➢ What decision have you made?

_____

_____

_____

Day 315: Galatians 1:1 – 24

Bible Study:

➢ Who is speaking? _____

➢ To whom is he speaking?

_____

➢ Put a squiggle line under how he praised God.

➢ Put stars next to his instructions.

➢ How does this apply to your life?

_____

_____

➢ Highlight a passage that speaks to you.

➢ Write a thought God gave to you.

_____

_____

_____

Prayer Prompts:

➢ Praise God by saying, "Glory to God."

➢ Confess something God has laid on your heart.

➢ Confess sins you committed today.

➢ Pray for people in your church.

➢ Pray for the needs of someone else.

➢ Pray for something you need today.

Decision:

➢ What decision have you made?

_____

_____

_____

Day 316: Galatians 6:1 – 10

Bible Study:

➢ Underline and define words you do not know.

_____

_____

_____

➢ Put an arrow next to each of the nice things we are supposed to do for others.

➢ Put an exclamation point (!) next to the pride.

➢ How does this apply to your life?

_____

_____

_____

➢ Highlight a passage that speaks to you.

➢ Write a thought God gave to you.

_____

_____

_____

➢ Memorize verse 7 – 9.

Prayer Prompts:

➢ Praise God for blessing our efforts.

➢ Confess something God has laid on your heart.

➢ Confess sins you committed today.

➢ Pray for something God has laid on your heart.

➢ Pray for the needs of someone else.

➢ Pray for something you need today.

Decision:

➢ What decision have you made?

_____

_____

_____

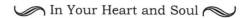

Day 317: Acts 18:1 – 17

Bible Study:

➤ Underline and define words you do not know.

_____

_____

_____

➤ Look up this location.

➤ Put an exclamation point (!) next to how the Jews responded to Paul.

➤ Double underline God's words.

➤ Circle Paul's obedience.

➤ How does this apply to your life?

_____

_____

➤ Highlight a passage that speaks to you.

➤ Write a thought God gave to you.

_____

_____

_____

Prayer Prompts:

➤ Praise God for guiding your life.

➤ Confess something God has laid on your heart.

➤ Confess sins you committed today.

➤ Pray for a mission field.

➤ Pray for the needs of someone else.

➤ Pray for something you need today.

Decision:

➤ What decision have you made?

_____

_____

_____

Day 318: 1 Thessalonians 1:1 & 3:1 – 13

Bible Study:

➤ Who is speaking? _____

➤ To whom is he speaking? _____

➤ Circle why Timotheus was sent.

➤ Circle the faith of the Thessalonians.

➤ Put a squiggle line under the names of God.

➤ How does this apply to your life?

_____

_____

_____

_____

_____

➤ Highlight a passage that speaks to you.

➤ Write a thought God gave to you.

_____

_____

_____

Prayer Prompts:

➤ Praise God for encouraging friends.

➤ Confess something God has laid on your heart.

➤ Confess sins you committed today.

➤ Pray for something God has laid on your heart.

➤ Pray for the needs of someone else.

➤ Pray for something you need today.

Decision:

➤ What decision have you made?

_____

_____

_____

Day 319: 1 Thessalonians 5:1 – 11

Bible Study:

➢ What is the day of the Lord?

_____

➢ When is the day of the Lord?

_____

➢ How can we prepare for the day of the Lord?

_____

_____

➢ How does this apply to your life?

_____

_____

➢ Highlight a passage that speaks to you.

➢ Write a thought God gave to you.

_____

_____

_____

➢ Memorize verse 5.

Prayer Prompts:

➢ Praise God for the second coming.

➢ Confess something God has laid on your heart.

➢ Confess sins you committed today.

➢ Pray for people that need to be saved.

➢ Pray for the needs of someone else.

➢ Pray for something you need today.

Decision:

➢ What decision have you made?

_____

_____

_____

Day 320: 2 Thessalonians 2:1 – 17

Bible Study:

➢ Underline and define words you do not know.

_____

_____

➢ Put an exclamation point (!) next to the sins.

➢ Put an X next to the result.

➢ Put a squiggle line under why God is praised.

➢ Put a star next to the instructions.

➢ How does this apply to your life?

_____

_____

_____

➢ Highlight a passage that speaks to you.

➢ Write a thought God gave to you.

_____

_____

_____

Prayer Prompts:

➢ Praise God using the multiple names of God.

➢ Confess something God has laid on your heart.

➢ Confess sins you committed today.

➢ Pray for something God has laid on your heart.

➢ Pray for the needs of someone else.

➢ Pray for something you need today.

Decision:

➢ What decision have you made?

_____

_____

_____

Day 321: 1 Corinthians 1:1 – 2, 10 – 31

Bible Study:

➢ Who is speaking? _____

➢ To whom is he speaking? _____

➢ Put a squiggle line under the names of Jesus.

➢ Put a star next to the instructions.

➢ What was the argument about?

_____

➢ What was Paul's response?

_____

➢ How does this apply to your life?

_____

_____

_____

➢ Highlight a passage that speaks to you.

➢ Write a thought God gave to you.

_____

_____

Prayer Prompts:

➢ Praise God by giving glory to His name.

➢ Confess something God has laid on your heart.

➢ Confess sins you committed today.

➢ Pray for something God has laid on your heart.

➢ Pray for the needs of someone else.

➢ Pray for something you need today.

Decision:

➢ What decision have you made?

_____

_____

_____

Day 322: 1 Corinthians 9:18 – 26

Bible Study:

➢ Put a star next to the instructions.

➢ What is the race and fight we are in?

_____

_____

➢ What reward will we win?

_____

➢ How does this apply to your life?

_____

_____

_____

➢ Highlight a passage that speaks to you.

➢ Write a thought God gave to you.

_____

_____

_____

➢ Memorize verse 24.

Prayer Prompts:

➢ Praise God for our reward in Heaven.

➢ Confess something God has laid on your heart.

➢ Confess sins you committed today.

➢ Pray for something God has laid on your heart.

➢ Pray for the needs of someone else.

➢ Pray for something you need today.

Decision:

➢ What decision have you made?

_____

_____

_____

Day 323: 1 Corinthians 12:1 – 11

Bible Study:

- ➤ Put a squiggle line under the names of Jesus.
- ➤ What are the gifts?

_____

_____

- ➤ What gift do you have?

_____

_____

- ➤ How does this apply to your life?

_____

_____

_____

- ➤ Highlight a passage that speaks to you.
- ➤ Write a thought God gave to you.

_____

_____

_____

Prayer Prompts:

- ➤ Praise God for your special gift.
- ➤ Confess something God has laid on your heart.
- ➤ Confess sins you committed today.
- ➤ Pray for something God has laid on your heart.
- ➤ Pray for the needs of someone else.
- ➤ Pray for something you need today.

Decision:

- ➤ What decision have you made?

_____

_____

_____

Day 324: 1 Corinthians 12:12 – 31

Bible Study:

➢ Underline and define words you do not know.

_____

_____

➢ What is the body? _____

➢ Who are the members? _____

➢ Which member is the most important?

_____

_____

➢ How does this apply to your life?

_____

_____

_____

➢ Highlight a passage that speaks to you.

➢ Write a thought God gave to you.

_____

_____

Prayer Prompts:

➢ Praise God for the members of your church.

➢ Confess something God has laid on your heart.

➢ Confess sins you committed today.

➢ Pray for something God has laid on your heart.

➢ Pray for the needs of someone else.

➢ Pray for something you need today.

Decision:

➢ What decision have you made?

_____

_____

_____

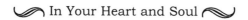

Day 325: 1 Corinthians 13:1 – 13

Bible Study:

➤ Underline and define words you do not know.

_____

_____

➤ Circle the Biblical traits.

➤ What is the best trait to have?

_____

_____

➤ How does this apply to your life?

_____

_____

_____

➤ Highlight a passage that speaks to you.

➤ Write a thought God gave to you.

_____

_____

➤ Memorize verse 13.

Prayer Prompts:

➤ Praise God for His love.

➤ Confess something God has laid on your heart.

➤ Confess sins you committed today.

➤ Pray for something God has laid on your heart.

➤ Pray for the needs of someone else.

➤ Pray for something you need today.

Decision:

➤ What decision have you made?

_____

_____

_____

Day 326: 2 Corinthians 7:1 – 16

Bible Study:

➢ Underline and define words you do not know.

_____

_____

_____

➢ Circle the comfort the Corinthians gave.

➢ How does this apply to your life?

_____

_____

_____

➢ Highlight a passage that speaks to you.

➢ Write a thought God gave to you.

_____

_____

➢ Memorize verse 16.

Prayer Prompts:

➢ Praise God for friends that comfort you.

➢ Confess something God has laid on your heart.

➢ Confess sins you committed today.

➢ Pray for something God has laid on your heart.

➢ Pray for the needs of someone else.

➢ Pray for something you need today.

Decision:

➢ What decision have you made?

_____

_____

_____

Day 327: 2 Corinthians 9:1 – 15

Bible Study:

- ➢ Put an exclamation point (!) next to the sins.
- ➢ Circle the Biblical traits.
- ➢ Put a squiggle line under the praise and prayers.
- ➢ Put an arrow next to the giving.
- ➢ Put an X next to what happens if you give.
- ➢ How does this apply to your life?

_____

_____

_____

- ➢ Highlight a passage that speaks to you.
- ➢ Write a thought God gave to you.

_____

_____

_____

- ➢ Memorize verse 6.

Prayer Prompts:

- ➢ Praise God for His gifts to you.
- ➢ Confess something God has laid on your heart.
- ➢ Confess sins you committed today.
- ➢ Pray for something God has laid on your heart.
- ➢ Pray for the needs of someone else.
- ➢ Pray for something you need today.

Decision:

- ➢ What decision have you made?

_____

_____

_____

Day 328: Romans 3:1 – 23

Bible Study:

➢ What are the characteristics of God?

_____

_____

_____

➢ Put an exclamation point (!) next to the sins.

➢ How does this apply to your life?

_____

_____

_____

➢ Highlight a passage that speaks to you.

➢ Write a thought God gave to you.

_____

_____

_____

➢ Memorize verse 23.

Prayer Prompts:

➢ Praise Jesus for dying for your sins.

➢ Confess something God has laid on your heart.

➢ Confess sins you committed today.

➢ Pray for something God has laid on your heart.

➢ Pray for the needs of someone else.

➢ Pray for something you need today.

Decision:

➢ What decision have you made?

_____

_____

_____

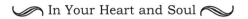

Day 329: Romans 6:1 – 23

Bible Study:

➤ If everyone is a sinner, why should you try not to sin?

_____

_____

_____

➤ Put stars next to the instructions.

➤ How does this apply to your life?

_____

_____

_____

➤ Highlight a passage that speaks to you.

➤ Write a thought God gave to you.

_____

_____

_____

➤ Memorize verse 23.

Prayer Prompts:

➤ Praise Jesus for the gift of eternal life.

➤ Confess something God has laid on your heart.

➤ Confess sins you committed today.

➤ Pray for something God has laid on your heart.

➤ Pray for the needs of someone else.

➤ Pray for something you need today.

Decision:

➤ What decision have you made?

_____

_____

_____

Day 330: Romans 10:1 – 21

Bible Study:

➤ How does someone get saved?

_____

_____

_____

_____

_____

➤ How does this apply to your life?

_____

_____

_____

➤ Highlight a passage that speaks to you.

➤ Write a thought God gave to you.

_____

_____

_____

➤ Memorize verses 9 & 13.

Prayer Prompts:

➤ Praise God for salvation.

➤ Confess something God has laid on your heart.

➤ Confess sins you committed today.

➤ Pray for something God has laid on your heart.

➤ Pray for the needs of someone else.

➤ Pray for something you need today.

Decision:

➤ What decision have you made?

_____

_____

_____

Day 331: Romans 12:1 – 21

Bible Study:

➢ Underline and define words you do not know.

_____

_____

_____

➢ Circle the Biblical traits.

➢ Put stars next to the instructions.

➢ How does this apply to your life?

_____

_____

_____

➢ Highlight a passage that speaks to you.

➢ Write a thought God gave to you.

_____

_____

➢ Memorize verses 1 – 2.

Prayer Prompts:

➢ Praise God for grace.

➢ Confess something God has laid on your heart.

➢ Confess sins you committed today.

➢ Pray for something God has laid on your heart.

➢ Pray for the needs of someone else.

➢ Pray for something you need today.

Decision:

➢ What decision have you made?

_____

_____

_____

Day 332: Acts 21:27 – 36

Bible Study:

➤ Put an exclamation point (!) next to the sins of the Jews in Asia.

➤ How did Paul respond?

_____

_____

_____

➤ How does this apply to your life?

_____

_____

_____

➤ Highlight a passage that speaks to you.

➤ Write a thought God gave to you.

_____

_____

_____

Prayer Prompts:

➤ Praise God for something special in your life.

➤ Confess something God has laid on your heart.

➤ Confess sins you committed today.

➤ Pray for something God has laid on your heart.

➤ Pray for the needs of someone else.

➤ Pray for something you need today.

Decision:

➤ What decision have you made?

_____

_____

_____

Day 333: Acts 24:10 – 27

Bible Study:

➢ How did Paul defend himself?

_____

_____

_____

➢ Circle the Biblical traits.

➢ How does this apply to your life?

_____

_____

_____

➢ Highlight a passage that speaks to you.

➢ Write a thought God gave to you.

_____

_____

_____

Prayer Prompts:

➢ Praise God as your Father.

➢ Confess something God has laid on your heart.

➢ Confess sins you committed today.

➢ Pray for something God has laid on your heart.

➢ Pray for the needs of someone else.

➢ Pray for something you need today.

Decision:

➢ What decision have you made?

_____

_____

_____

Day 334: Acts 25:1 – 12

Bible Study:

➤ Put an exclamation point (!) next to the sins.

➤ How did Paul defend himself?

_____

_____

_____

➤ How does this apply to your life?

_____

_____

_____

➤ Highlight a passage that speaks to you.

➤ Write a thought God gave to you.

_____

_____

_____

Prayer Prompts:

➤ Praise God for something you see.

➤ Confess something God has laid on your heart.

➤ Confess sins you committed today.

➤ Pray for something God has laid on your heart.

➤ Pray for the needs of someone else.

➤ Pray for something you need today.

Decision:

➤ What decision have you made?

_____

_____

_____

Day 335: Acts 25:13 – 27

Bible Study:

➤ Underline and define words you do not know.

_____

_____

➤ How many trials did Paul have? _____

➤ What was the result of the trials?

_____

_____

➤ How does this apply to your life?

_____

_____

_____

➤ Highlight a passage that speaks to you.

➤ Write a thought God gave to you.

_____

_____

_____

Prayer Prompts:

➤ Praise God for a miracle in your life.

➤ Confess something God has laid on your heart.

➤ Confess sins you committed today.

➤ Pray for something God has laid on your heart.

➤ Pray for the needs of someone else.

➤ Pray for something you need today.

Decision:

➤ What decision have you made?

_____

_____

_____

Day 336: Acts 27:1 – 22

Bible Study:

➢ Underline and define words you do not know.

_____

_____

_____

➢ Look up a map of this area.
➢ How does this apply to your life?

_____

_____

_____

➢ Highlight a passage that speaks to you.
➢ Write a thought God gave to you.

_____

_____

_____

Prayer Prompts:

➢ Praise God for something on your mind.
➢ Confess something God has laid on your heart.
➢ Confess sins you committed today.
➢ Pray for something God has laid on your heart.
➢ Pray for the needs of someone else.
➢ Pray for a mission field.
➢ Pray for something you need today.

Decision:

➢ What decision have you made?

_____

_____

_____

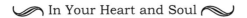 In Your Heart and Soul

Day 337: Acts 27:23 – 44

Bible Study:

➤ Underline and define words you do not know.

_____

_____

_____

➤ Put a squiggle line under how they prayed and praised.

➤ Put an exclamation point (!) next to what the soldiers wanted to do.

➤ Double star the miracles.

➤ How does this apply to your life?

_____

_____

_____

➤ Highlight a passage that speaks to you.

➤ Write a thought God gave to you.

_____

_____

_____

Prayer Prompts:

➤ Praise God for helping you through a storm.

➤ Confess something God has laid on your heart.

➤ Confess sins you committed today.

➤ Pray for something God has laid on your heart.

➤ Pray for the needs of someone else.

➤ Pray for something you need today.

Decision:

➤ What decision have you made?

_____

_____

_____

Day 338: Colossians 1:1 – 2 & 2:1 – 23

Bible Study:

➢ Who is speaking? _____

➢ To whom is he speaking? _____

➢ Put a squiggle line under how Paul praised God.

➢ Put stars next to the instructions.

➢ Double star the miracles.

➢ How does this apply to your life?

_____

_____

_____

➢ Highlight a passage that speaks to you.

➢ Write a thought God gave to you.

_____

_____

_____

➢ Memorize verse 6 – 7.

Prayer Prompts:

➢ Praise God for something on your mind.

➢ Confess something God has laid on your heart.

➢ Confess sins you committed today.

➢ Pray for something God has laid on your heart.

➢ Pray for the needs of someone else.

➢ Pray for a mission field.

➢ Pray for something you need today.

Decision:

➢ What decision have you made?

_____

_____

_____

Day 339: Colossians 4:1 – 18

Bible Study:

➤ Underline and define words you do not know.

_____

_____

_____

➤ Put a squiggle line under the praises and prayers.

➤ Put stars next to the instructions.

➤ How does this apply to your life?

_____

_____

_____

➤ Highlight a passage that speaks to you.

➤ Write a thought God gave to you.

_____

_____

_____

Prayer Prompts:

➤ Praise God for your pastor.

➤ Confess something God has laid on your heart.

➤ Confess sins you committed today.

➤ Pray for something God has laid on your heart.

➤ Pray for the needs of someone else.

➤ Pray for something you need today.

Decision:

➤ What decision have you made?

_____

_____

_____

Day 340: Philemon 1:1 – 2, 8 – 25

Bible Study:

➤ Who is speaking? _____

➤ To whom is he speaking? _____

➤ Put an exclamation point (!) next to what Onesimus did wrong.

➤ Put an arrow next to Paul's kindness.

➤ Put a squiggle line under how Paul praised Jesus.

➤ How does this apply to your life?

_____

_____

_____

➤ Highlight a passage that speaks to you.

➤ Write a thought God gave to you.

_____

_____

_____

Prayer Prompts:

➤ Praise God for something on your mind.

➤ Confess something God has laid on your heart.

➤ Confess sins you committed today.

➤ Pray for something God has laid on your heart.

➤ Pray for the needs of someone else.

➤ Pray for something you need today.

Decision:

➤ What decision have you made?

_____

_____

_____

Day 341: Ephesians 3:1:1 & 3:1 – 17

Bible Study:

➤ Who is speaking? _____

➤ To whom is he speaking? _____

➤ Put stars next to the instructions.

➤ Put a squiggle line under the praises and prayers.

➤ How does this apply to your life?

_____

_____

_____

➤ Highlight a passage that speaks to you.

➤ Write a thought God gave to you.

_____

_____

_____

➤ Memorize verse 17.

Prayer Prompts:

➤ Praise God for something on your mind.

➤ Confess something God has laid on your heart.

➤ Confess sins you committed today.

➤ Pray for something God has laid on your heart.

➤ Pray for the needs of someone else.

➤ Pray for something you need today.

Decision:

➤ What decision have you made?

_____

_____

_____

Day 342: Ephesians 4:1 – 16

Bible Study:

➢ Underline and define words you do not know.

_____

_____

➢ Put stars next to the instructions.

➢ Put a squiggle line under the praises and prayers.

➢ How does this apply to your life?

_____

_____

_____

➢ Highlight a passage that speaks to you.

➢ Write a thought God gave to you.

_____

_____

_____

➢ Memorize verse 4.

Prayer Prompts:

➢ Praise God for something on your mind.

➢ Confess something God has laid on your heart.

➢ Confess sins you committed today.

➢ Pray for something God has laid on your heart.

➢ Pray for the needs of someone else.

➢ Pray for a mission field.

➢ Pray for something you need today.

Decision:

➢ What decision have you made?

_____

_____

_____

Day 343: Ephesians 5:21 – 6:9

Bible Study:

➤ Underline and define words you do not know.

_____

_____

_____

➤ Put stars next to the instructions.

➤ How does this apply to your life?

_____

_____

_____

➤ Highlight a passage that speaks to you.

➤ Write a thought God gave to you.

_____

_____

_____

➤ Memorize verses 1 – 4.

Prayer Prompts:

➤ Praise God for something on your mind.

➤ Confess something God has laid on your heart.

➤ Confess sins you committed today.

➤ Pray for something God has laid on your heart.

➤ Pray for the needs of someone else.

➤ Pray for something you need today.

Decision:

➤ What decision have you made?

_____

_____

_____

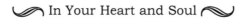

Day 344: Ephesians 6:10 – 20

Bible Study:

➢ Underline and define words you do not know.

_____

_____

➢ Put stars next to the instructions.

➢ Put a squiggle line under how to pray.

➢ How does this apply to your life?

_____

_____

_____

➢ Highlight a passage that speaks to you.

➢ Write a thought God gave to you.

_____

_____

_____

➢ Memorize verses 13 – 17.

Prayer Prompts:

➢ Praise God for something on your mind.

➢ Confess something God has laid on your heart.

➢ Confess sins you committed today.

➢ Pray for something God has laid on your heart.

➢ Pray for the needs of someone else.

➢ Pray for a mission field.

➢ Pray for something you need today.

Decision:

➢ What decision have you made?

_____

_____

_____

Day 345: Philippians 1:1 – 3 & 2:1 – 11

Bible Study:

➤ Who is speaking? _____

➤ To whom is he speaking? _____

➤ Put a squiggle line under the praises.

➤ Put an exclamation point (!) next to the comparisons.

➤ Put stars next to the instructions.

➤ How does this apply to your life?

_____

_____

_____

➤ Highlight a passage that speaks to you.

➤ Write a thought God gave to you.

_____

_____

_____

➤ Memorize verses 5 – 9.

Prayer Prompts:

➤ Praise God for something on your mind.

➤ Confess something God has laid on your heart.

➤ Confess sins you committed today.

➤ Pray for something God has laid on your heart.

➤ Pray for the needs of someone else.

➤ Pray for something you need today.

Decision:

➤ What decision have you made?

_____

_____

_____

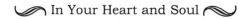

Day 346: Philippians 3:1 – 16

Bible Study:

➤ Underline and define words you do not know.

_____

_____

_____

➤ Put stars next to the instructions.

➤ How does this apply to your life?

_____

_____

_____

➤ Highlight a passage that speaks to you.

➤ Write a thought God gave to you.

_____

_____

_____

➤ Memorize verses 13 – 14.

Prayer Prompts:

➤ Praise God for something on your mind.

➤ Confess something God has laid on your heart.

➤ Confess sins you committed today.

➤ Pray for something God has laid on your heart.

➤ Pray for the needs of someone else.

➤ Pray for a mission field.

➤ Pray for something you need today.

Decision:

➤ What decision have you made?

_____

_____

_____

Day 347: 1 Timothy 1:1 – 2 & 2:1 – 8

Bible Study:

➤ Underline and define words you do not know.

_____

_____

➤ Who is speaking? _____

➤ To whom is he speaking? _____

➤ Put a squiggle line under how to pray.

➤ How does this apply to your life?

_____

_____

_____

➤ Highlight a passage that speaks to you.

➤ Write a thought God gave to you.

_____

_____

_____

➤ Memorize verse 5.

Prayer Prompts:

➤ Praise God for something on your mind.

➤ Confess something God has laid on your heart.

➤ Confess sins you committed today.

➤ Pray for something God has laid on your heart.

➤ Pray for the needs of someone else.

➤ Pray for something you need today.

Decision:

➤ What decision have you made?

_____

_____

_____

Day 348: 1 Timothy 6:6 – 21

Bible Study:

➢ Underline and define words you do not know.

_____

_____

➢ Put stars next to the instructions.

➢ Put an exclamation point (!) next to the sins.

➢ Put a squiggle line under the praises.

➢ How does this apply to your life?

_____

_____

_____

➢ Highlight a passage that speaks to you.

➢ Write a thought God gave to you.

_____

_____

_____

➢ Memorize verses 6 & 10.

Prayer Prompts:

➢ Praise God for something on your mind.

➢ Confess something God has laid on your heart.

➢ Confess sins you committed today.

➢ Pray for something God has laid on your heart.

➢ Pray for the needs of someone else.

➢ Pray for something you need today.

Decision:

➢ What decision have you made?

_____

_____

_____

Day 349: Titus 1:1 – 4 & 2:1 – 15

Bible Study:

➤ Who is speaking? _____

➤ To whom is he speaking? _____

➤ Put stars next to the instructions.

➤ Put a squiggle line under the praises.

➤ How does this apply to your life?

_____

_____

_____

➤ Highlight a passage that speaks to you.

➤ Write a thought God gave to you.

_____

_____

_____

➤ Memorize verses 13 – 14.

Prayer Prompts:

➤ Praise God for something on your mind.

➤ Confess something God has laid on your heart.

➤ Confess sins you committed today.

➤ Pray for something God has laid on your heart.

➤ Pray for the needs of someone else.

➤ Pray for something you need today.

Decision:

➤ What decision have you made?

_____

_____

_____

Day 350: 1 Peter 1:1 – 21

Bible Study:

➤ Who is speaking? _____

➤ To whom is he speaking? _____

➤ Put a squiggle line under the praises.

➤ Put stars next to the instructions.

➤ How does this apply to your life?

_____

_____

_____

➤ Highlight a passage that speaks to you.

➤ Write a thought God gave to you.

_____

_____

_____

➤ Memorize verse 16.

Prayer Prompts:

➤ Praise God for something on your mind.

➤ Confess something God has laid on your heart.

➤ Confess sins you committed today.

➤ Pray for something God has laid on your heart.

➤ Pray for the needs of someone else.

➤ Pray for a mission field.

➤ Pray for something you need today.

Decision:

➤ What decision have you made?

_____

_____

_____

Day 351: 1 Peter 2:1 – 12

Bible Study:

➢ What are the stones? _____

➢ Put an exclamation point (!) next to the sins.

➢ Put stars next to the instructions.

➢ How does this apply to your life?

_____

_____

_____

➢ Highlight a passage that speaks to you.

➢ Write a thought God gave to you.

_____

_____

_____

➢ Memorize verse 9.

Prayer Prompts:

➢ Praise God for something on your mind.

➢ Confess something God has laid on your heart.

➢ Confess sins you committed today.

➢ Pray for something God has laid on your heart.

➢ Pray for the needs of someone else.

➢ Pray for a mission field.

➢ Pray for something you need today.

Decision:

➢ What decision have you made?

_____

_____

_____

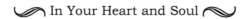

Day 352: 1 Peter 5:1 – 11

Bible Study:

➤ Underline and define words you do not know.

_____

_____

➤ Put stars next to the instructions.

➤ Put a squiggle line under the praises.

➤ How does this apply to your life?

_____

_____

_____

➤ Highlight a passage that speaks to you.

➤ Write a thought God gave to you.

_____

_____

_____

➤ Memorize verses 6 – 7.

Prayer Prompts:

➤ Praise God for something on your mind.

➤ Confess something God has laid on your heart.

➤ Confess sins you committed today.

➤ Pray for something God has laid on your heart.

➤ Pray for the needs of someone else.

➤ Pray for a mission field.

➤ Pray for something you need today.

Decision:

➤ What decision have you made?

_____

_____

_____

Day 353: Hebrews 1:1 – 14

Bible Study:

➢ Put a squiggle line under the praises.

➢ Who is superior: Jesus or the angels?

_____

_____

➢ How does this apply to your life?

_____

_____

_____

➢ Highlight a passage that speaks to you.

➢ Write a thought God gave to you.

_____

_____

Prayer Prompts:

➢ Praise God for something on your mind.

➢ Confess something God has laid on your heart.

➢ Confess sins you committed today.

➢ Pray for something God has laid on your heart.

➢ Pray for the needs of someone else.

➢ Pray for a mission field.

➢ Pray for something you need today.

Decision:

➢ What decision have you made?

_____

_____

_____

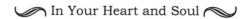

Day 354: Hebrews 11:1 – 20

Bible Study:

➢   Underline and define words you do not know.

_____

_____

_____

➢   Circle the faith of each person.

➢   How does this apply to your life?

_____

_____

_____

➢   Highlight a passage that speaks to you.

➢   Write a thought God gave to you.

_____

_____

_____

➢   Memorize verse 1.

Prayer Prompts:

➢   Praise God for something on your mind.

➢   Confess something God has laid on your heart.

➢   Confess sins you committed today.

➢   Pray for something God has laid on your heart.

➢   Pray for the needs of someone else.

➢   Pray for a mission field.

➢   Pray for something you need today.

Decision:

➢   What decision have you made?

_____

_____

_____

Day 355: Hebrews 11:21 – 40

Bible Study:

➢ Underline and define words you do not know.

_____

_____

_____

➢ Circle the faith of each person.

➢ How does this apply to your life?

_____

_____

_____

➢ Highlight a passage that speaks to you.

➢ Write a thought God gave to you.

_____

_____

_____

Prayer Prompts:

➢ Praise God for something on your mind.

➢ Confess something God has laid on your heart.

➢ Confess sins you committed today.

➢ Pray for something God has laid on your heart.

➢ Pray for the needs of someone else.

➢ Pray for a mission field.

➢ Pray for something you need today.

Decision:

➢ What decision have you made?

_____

_____

_____

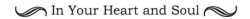

Day 356: 2 Timothy :1 – 14

Bible Study:

➤ Underline and define words you do not know.

_____

_____

➤ Who is speaking? _____

➤ To whom is he speaking? _____

➤ Put a squiggle line under the praises.

➤ Put an arrow next to the encouragement.

➤ How does this apply to your life?

_____

_____

➤ Highlight a passage that speaks to you.

➤ Write a thought God gave to you.

_____

_____

➤ Memorize verse 7.

Prayer Prompts:

➤ Praise God for something on your mind.

➤ Confess something God has laid on your heart.

➤ Confess sins you committed today.

➤ Pray for something God has laid on your heart.

➤ Pray for the needs of someone else.

➤ Pray for a mission field.

➤ Pray for something you need today.

Decision:

➤ What decision have you made?

_____

_____

_____

Day 357: 2 Peter 2:1 – 15

Bible Study:

➢ Who is speaking? _____

➢ To whom is he speaking? _____

➢ Put an exclamation point (!) next to the sins.

➢ Put an X next to the results.

➢ How does this apply to your life?

_____

_____

_____

➢ Highlight a passage that speaks to you.

➢ Write a thought God gave to you.

_____

_____

_____

Prayer Prompts:

➢ Praise God for something on your mind.

➢ Confess something God has laid on your heart.

➢ Confess sins you committed today.

➢ Pray for something God has laid on your heart.

➢ Pray for the needs of someone else.

➢ Pray for a mission field.

➢ Pray for something you need today.

Decision:

➢ What decision have you made?

_____

_____

_____

Day 358: Jude 1:1 – 25

Bible Study:

➤ Who is speaking? _____

➤ To whom is he speaking? _____

➤ Put an exclamation point (!) next to the sins.

➤ How does this apply to your life?

_____

_____

_____

➤ Highlight a passage that speaks to you.

➤ Write a thought God gave to you.

_____

_____

_____

➤ Memorize verse 22.

Prayer Prompts:

➤ Praise God for something on your mind.

➤ Confess something God has laid on your heart.

➤ Confess sins you committed today.

➤ Pray for something God has laid on your heart.

➤ Pray for the needs of someone else.

➤ Pray for a mission field.

➤ Pray for something you need today.

Decision:

➤ What decision have you made?

_____

_____

_____

Day 359: 1 John 1:1 – 10

Bible Study:

➢ Put an exclamation point (!) next to the sins.

➢ Put stars next to the instructions.

➢ Put a squiggle line under the names of God.

➢ How does this apply to your life?

_____

_____

_____

➢ Highlight a passage that speaks to you.

➢ Write a thought God gave to you.

_____

_____

_____

➢ Memorize verses 4 – 10.

Prayer Prompts:

➢ Praise God for something on your mind.

➢ Confess something God has laid on your heart.

➢ Confess sins you committed today.

➢ Pray for something God has laid on your heart.

➢ Pray for the needs of someone else.

➢ Pray for a mission field.

➢ Pray for something you need today.

Decision:

➢ What decision have you made?

_____

_____

_____

Day 360: 2 John 1:1 – 13

Bible Study:

➤ Who is speaking? _____

➤ To whom is he speaking? _____

➤ Put stars next to the instructions.

➤ How does this apply to your life?

_____

_____

_____

➤ Highlight a passage that speaks to you.

➤ Write a thought God gave to you.

_____

_____

_____

➤ Pick a verse to memorize.

Prayer Prompts:

➤ Praise God for something on your mind.

➤ Confess something God has laid on your heart.

➤ Confess sins you committed today.

➤ Pray for something God has laid on your heart.

➤ Pray for the needs of someone else.

➤ Pray for a mission field.

➤ Pray for something you need today.

Decision:

➤ What decision have you made?

_____

_____

_____

Day 361: 3 John 1:1 – 14

Bible Study:

- ➤ Who is speaking? _____
- ➤ To whom is he speaking? _____
- ➤ Put stars next to the instructions.
- ➤ How does this apply to your life?

  _____

  _____

  _____

- ➤ Highlight a passage that speaks to you.
- ➤ Write a thought God gave to you.

  _____

  _____

  _____

- ➤ Memorize verse 4.

Prayer Prompts:

- ➤ Praise God for something on your mind.
- ➤ Confess something God has laid on your heart.
- ➤ Confess sins you committed today.
- ➤ Pray for something God has laid on your heart.
- ➤ Pray for the needs of someone else.
- ➤ Pray for a mission field.
- ➤ Pray for something you need today.

Decision:

- ➤ What decision have you made?

  _____

  _____

  _____

Day 362: Revelation 1:1 – 20

Bible Study:

➤ Who is speaking? _____

➤ To whom is he speaking? _____

➤ Double underline Jesus' words.

➤ Put a squiggle line under how John worshiped.

➤ What are the seven stars and seven candlesticks? _____

➤ How does this apply to your life?

_____

_____

➤ Highlight a passage that speaks to you.

➤ Write a thought God gave to you.

_____

_____

_____

➤ Pick a verse to memorize.

Prayer Prompts:

➤ Praise God for something on your mind.

➤ Confess something God has laid on your heart.

➤ Confess sins you committed today.

➤ Pray for something God has laid on your heart.

➤ Pray for the needs of someone else.

➤ Pray for a mission field.

➤ Pray for something you need today.

Decision:

➤ What decision have you made?

_____

_____

_____

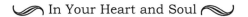

Day 363: Revelation 5:1 – 14

Bible Study:

- ➤ Put a squiggle line under the names of God and how He was praised.

- ➤ Who has the power to open the book? _____

- ➤ How does this apply to your life?

  _____

  _____

  _____

- ➤ Highlight a passage that speaks to you.

- ➤ Write a thought God gave to you.

  _____

  _____

  _____

- ➤ What questions do you have?

  _____

  _____

  _____

Prayer Prompts:

- ➤ Praise God for something on your mind.

- ➤ Confess something God has laid on your heart.

- ➤ Confess sins you committed today.

- ➤ Pray for something God has laid on your heart.

- ➤ Pray for the needs of someone else.

- ➤ Pray for a mission field.

- ➤ Pray for something you need today.

Decision:

- ➤ What decision have you made?

  _____

  _____

  _____

Day 364: Revelation 20:1 – 15

Bible Study:

➤ Underline and define words you do not know.

_____

_____

_____

➤ Who is the dragon? _____

➤ Put an X next to what will happen to him.

➤ What are the books?

_____

_____

_____

➤ Put an X next to what will happen to those not found in the book of life.

➤ How does this apply to your life?

_____

_____

_____

➤ Highlight a passage that speaks to you.

➤ Write a thought God gave to you.

_____

_____

_____

➤ What questions do you have?

_____

_____

_____

Prayer Prompts:

➤ Praise God for something on your mind.

➤ Confess something God has laid on your heart.

➤ Confess sins you committed today.

➤ Pray for something God has laid on your heart.

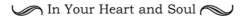

➢ Pray for the needs of someone else.

➢ Pray for a mission field.

➢ Pray for something you need today.

Decision:

➢ What decision have you made?

_____

_____

_____

Day 365: Revelation 21:1 – 27

Bible Study:

➢ Put a box around God's actions.

➢ Double underline God's words.

➢ How does this apply to your life?

_____

_____

_____

➢ Highlight a passage that speaks to you.

➢ Write a thought God gave to you.

_____

_____

➢ What questions do you have?

_____

_____

➢ Pick a verse to memorize.

Prayer Prompts:

➢ Praise God for something on your mind.

➢ Confess something God has laid on your heart.

➢ Confess sins you committed today.

➢ Pray for something God has laid on your heart.

➢ Pray for the needs of someone else.

➢ Pray for a mission field.

➢ Pray for something you need today.

Decision:

➢ What decision have you made?

_____

_____

_____

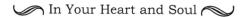

Day 366: Revelation 22:1 – 21

Bible Study:

➢ Underline and define words you do not know.

_____

_____

_____

➢ Put a squiggle line under the names of God and how He was praised.

➢ Double underline God's words.

➢ How does this apply to your life?

_____

_____

_____

➢ Highlight a passage that speaks to you.

➢ Write a thought God gave to you.

_____

_____

_____

➢ What questions do you have?

_____

_____

_____

➢ Pick a verse to memorize.

Prayer Prompts:

➢ Praise God for something on your mind.

➢ Confess something God has laid on your heart.

➢ Confess sins you committed today.

➢ Pray for something God has laid on your heart.

➢ Pray for the needs of someone else.

➢ Pray for a mission field.

➢ Pray for something you need today.

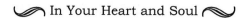

Decision:

➤ What decision have you made?

_____

_____

_____

Devotion Guide Reminders For Your Bible

- Ask Questions
    - o Who is speaking?
    - o To whom is he speaking?
    - o Who is the passage about?
    - o What is the passage about?
    - o Where is the passage set?
    - o When did the passage take place?
    - o How did those in the passage feel?
    - o Why did those in the passage make these decisions?
- Mark Your Bible
    - o Underline and Define words you do not know.
    - o Double underline God's/Jesus' words.
    - o Put a squiggle line under names of God, praises, prayers, or instructions about prayer.
    - o Put a star next to instructions or wisdom.
    - o Put two stars next to miracles.
    - o Circle Biblical characteristics.
    - o Put an exclamation point (!) next to sins.
    - o Put an X next to the effects from either the Biblical characteristics or the sinful actions.
- Apply It To Your Life
    - o Highlight a passage that speaks to you.
    - o Write about a personal experience.
    - o Write a thought God gave to you.
    - o Pick a verse to memorize.
    - o Write down questions you have.
    - o Write a decision you have made.
- Prayer Prompts
    - o Praise God for something on your mind.
    - o Confess something God has laid on your heart.
    - o Confess sins you committed today.
    - o Pray for something God has laid on your heart.
    - o Pray for the needs of someone else.
    - o Pray for a mission field.
    - o Pray for something you need today.

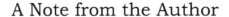

A Note from the Author

Dear Readers,

Thank you so much for reading! The love and support you have given me means more to me than you will ever know. I want to take this opportunity to tell you about something very important that happened to me. When I was little, I asked my parents how I could know for sure that I was going to go to Heaven. I would like to share with you what their answer was. They told me that the first thing I had to know was that I was a sinner. A sinner is someone who isn't perfect and sometimes does bad things. I knew even then that I sometimes did bad things. The next thing I needed to know was that being a sinner is what keeps us from going to Heaven. But thankfully, God wants everyone in Heaven, so He sent His Son, Jesus, to make a way for us to go to Heaven. When Jesus died on the cross, He paid for every bad thing we have ever done or will do. Now, anyone can go to Heaven if they only do one simple thing. They must believe that Jesus paid the price for their sin and accept the gift of going to Heaven. My parents helped me learn this and helped me pray a prayer accepting the gift to go to Heaven. The prayer went something like this: Dear Jesus, I know I do bad things, but I am accepting your gift to go to Heaven. Thank you, Jesus, Amen.

Sometimes I still sin, but I know that I am still going to go to Heaven because I accepted His free gift. You can pray that prayer too. I hope and pray that you will!

Thank you for reading this,

Kaitlyn King

Acknowledgements

I'd like to say thank you to Pastor King for helping me with the formatting of this devotion guide; and thank you to Hannah King, my ever-vigilant editor/best-older-sister-in-law-ever for correcting all of my mistakes.

I would also like to thank Loras Eymil for helping me with photographing the cover. I really appreciate it!

Finally, I'd like to give thanks to God for all He has done for me.

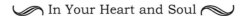

For More Information About Kaitlyn King:

Website: authorkaitlynking.com

Facebook Page: Author Kaitlyn King

Instagram: @authorkaitlynking

Also by Kaitlyn King:

Carried on a Christmas Wind

More than Conquerors, Book 1: The Forgotten Prince